THE
MONEY
SANDWICH

THE
MONEY
SANDWICH

A Complete Guide to Money, Family and Financial Freedom

MARC BINEHAM

WILEY

This edition first published in 2022 by John Wiley & Sons Australia, Ltd

42 McDougall St, Milton Qld 4064
Office also in Melbourne

Set in 10.5pt/14.5pt Caslon224Std by Straive, Chennai, India

ISBN: 978-1-119-91062-6

A catalogue record for this book is available from the National Library of Australia

Cover design by Alex Ross Creative

Cover image © VITTO-STUDIO/Shutterstock.com

Disclaimer
The material in this publication is of the nature of general comment only, and does not represent professional advice. It is not intended to provide specific guidance for particular circumstances and it should not be relied on as the basis for any decision to take action or not take action on any matter which it covers. Readers should obtain professional advice where appropriate, before making any such decision. To the maximum extent permitted by law, the author and publisher disclaim all responsibility and liability to any person, arising directly or indirectly from any person taking or not taking action based on the information in this publication.

Printed in Singapore
M122597_220622

To Anne-Maree, Katherine and Jacqui.

ACKNOWLEDGEMENT OF COUNTRY

I begin this book by acknowledging the Cammeraygal people, Traditional Custodians of the land on which I have lived and raised my family, and pay my respects to their Elders past and present.

ACKNOWLEDGEMENT OF CULTURE

I grew up in Australia in the 1960s and '70s, among children representing a diverse range of cultures. There were those from Italian, Greek and other European migrant families and others of my own proud Chinese heritage. I would like to acknowledge the sacrifices and courage of these families who have helped make Australia the welcoming and diverse country it is today.

Contents

Templates, calculators and other resource material referred to in this book are available to download from The Money Sandwich website:

Acknowledgements

Just a few people to thank as a book is never a one-person effort.

Thank you to Maree, Julie, Victoria and John for all their input and advice as we are all living in the 'sandwich generation'. My appreciation to Heather Kelly for her incredible editing skills and helpful hints. Thank you to Jaqui Lane and Debbie McInnes for their marketing skills in what's next for this book now published.

Thank you to my daughter Katherine for all the work she has done on the book; it was a massive effort and is very much appreciated.

I would like to make special mention of David Brewster, who helped me with this book. I wanted to avoid the number-one mistake of burying the reader in too much financial jargon. Fortuitously, David has had only a small amount of experience with financial advice himself and so was able to question me on assumptions I had made, which helped me change the language to what I believe is far more readable and user-friendly.

Finally, I would like to thank Lucy Raymond and the Wiley team for all their wonderful help and guidance. I look forward to a great partnership going forward.

About the author

 Marc Bineham joined the finance profession just over 30 years ago—memorably coinciding with the 1987 crash of the sharemarket. Despite the timing, he directed his knowledge and energy towards helping his very busy clients to have the best possible chance of reaching their financial and lifestyle goals.

Marc's light-bulb moment came early in his career when he was working with a couple in their early 60s and not far off retiring. He started the meeting explaining superannuation and its tax benefits, as well as discussing retirement projections. Their response was a simple but poignant comment: 'Marc, we don't get a second chance to retire. You need to get this right.' He was immediately reminded that this conversation was about more than just the numbers. It was about people.

From that point on, he has never forgotten that financial advice is a people and relationships business. They're still in contact with Marc today, even though he has now retired from financial advising to spend more time helping people as a money and retirement coach, speaker and author.

Marc is now part of the sandwich generation himself, and he believes people in this age group, along with their young adult children and elderly parents, all deserve a money and finance solution that is easy, affordable and provides continuing coaching for each step of the life journey.

Marc is a past national president of the Association of Financial Advisers (AFA) and has won numerous awards and recognition for his work. He enjoys speaking both in Australia and overseas on the topic of 'managing money better', and he sees an ongoing need for this in the community. His simple philosophy boils down to 'What's money for if not to provide a better life?'

Preface

After a career working for over 33 years in the financial advice industry, I can say with some confidence that Australians in general don't know enough about money. Some learn the basics of financial management at school, but after that it's pretty much a case of 'learn as you go'. This is not a good recipe for avoiding those keep-you-up-at-night moments that so many people experience at various points in their lives due to stress about money, and especially debt. Unfortunately, disagreements about money are also a significant factor in too many divorces.

Widespread lack of financial preparedness was demonstrated all too clearly during the COVID-19 pandemic. Many Australians were caught unawares, with many living pay-packet to pay-packet, while others experienced constant debt. Few had enough savings to cover two to three months of expenses. As a result, over 2.6 million Australians made withdrawals from their superannuation savings in order to make ends meet.

Effective management of money becomes both increasingly important and increasingly complex as you approach retirement age. This only increases stress levels more if you don't feel in control of the situation.

This book is my attempt to rectify this shortfall in knowledge and to guide members of the 'sandwich generation'—those predominantly in their 40s, 50s and 60s—through the financial matters that will affect them most in the years leading up to, and then after, their working life winding down. In writing it, I've drawn on the many real-life experiences I've had with my clients over three decades.

I'm also writing from a personal perspective. As a member of this generation myself, along with my wife and our friends, I understand the unique money issues our generation faces—what I call 'the money sandwich'. This is a great period of our lives, pre and early retirement, as we spend time with our adult children and our older and (for the most part) healthy parents. However, it does come with some unique money challenges. Aside from managing our own increasingly complex financial affairs, we're also thinking about how we can help our kids buy their first homes and how we might help our parents navigate the myriad (sometimes touchy) issues of aged care.

Two years ago, I was involved with David Koch at a consumer money expo, in my capacity with the Association of Financial Advisers (AFA). This provided a new perspective for me, as I met Australians who had never previously sought financial advice. These everyday mums and dads weren't asking about complex tax issues or transition-to-retirement superannuation strategies. Their questions were more like, 'Will I have enough to stop work one day?', 'How can I get my credit cards under control?' and 'How can I save, as I never seem to have anything left over?'

The Money Sandwich aims to provide some answers to your questions on both the basics of financial management in your 40s, 50s and 60s and on more complicated retirement planning. It also covers simple strategies you might implement on your own or with the help of your own adviser.

Of course, the best strategies in the world won't help if they are not implemented, so as much as this book is about creating a plan, you will need a way to keep yourself accountable. We're all human, and all have other things that can hold our attention. As I point out to many of my clients, even Roger Federer has a coach, and Bill Gates a mentor. Both recognise the benefits of being kept accountable. So I've also included a suggestion at the end of the book on the benefits of working with an adviser and how you can find one and work with them.

Marc Bineham

Introduction

Andrew and Rebecca are typical of many of the people who come to see me for financial advice. They're both in their 50s and have two kids: a son, Oliver, who's in the final year of a university degree, and a daughter, Maddie, who's in Year 12.

Andrew and Rebecca have always seemed to have enough money while never really getting ahead. Both have good jobs on decent salaries and they've been able to cover the mortgage payments on their suburban Sydney home, private school fees for both their children and the occasional overseas holiday, while maintaining what they regard as a comfortable but not extravagant lifestyle. They don't really budget, and they're not entirely sure what they spend their money on, but they seem to be able to keep their heads above water without too much trouble.

They've never sought financial advice because they've never felt the need to.

Their thinking is that, unless you win the lottery, you only need to see an adviser once you are retired, with a large lump sum from your superannuation fund to invest. They also believe that financial advisers are quite expensive.

Is this sounding familiar so far?

Andrew and Rebecca were out to dinner with a group of friends recently when the subject of retirement came up. An older couple in the group were talking about the income they generate from a couple of investment properties they own. Another couple, both of whom were self-employed, bemoaned the fact that they hardly have any superannuation savings and will probably have to work forever.

On the way home, Andrew and Rebecca realised that they had never really given all this any thought. While Andrew's father had died some years ago, his mother, in her early 70s, and Rebecca's parents, both nearly 80, were still going strong. Retirement and old age still seemed a long way off. It was partly for that reason that they had never got around to building any serious investments. Aside from their superannuation, built up through the compulsory super component of their salaries, they owned a few shares—and that was about it. Beyond maintaining their lifestyle, there had never been enough spare money or time to consider doing much else.

To put it simply, when it comes to money matters, Andrew and Rebecca have had the luxury of more or less coasting through life.

Now they face the prospect of a whole lot of uncertainty and change.

The kids will soon launch themselves into the 'real' world. Their parents are likely to need more care in the coming decade or so, if not sooner. And the prospect of retirement and life after work, and the financial implications of that, are no longer something they can simply ignore.

The sandwich generation

Andrew and Rebecca are typical of what I call the 'sandwich generation'. It's a generation of people in their 40s, 50s and 60s who are 'sandwiched' between their young adult or nearly adult children on one side and their ageing parents on the other. Just when they thought life might have been going to get a bit easier, they find themselves with a lot to think about.

Of course, the 'Andrews and Rebeccas' of the world come in many forms. Some members of the sandwich generation have higher incomes and some lower. Some are financially comfortable, at least on the surface, while for others being financially stressed is a day-to-day reality. Some have substantial investments behind them, while others have carried a high level of debt for many years. (We'll come back to this, but let me make the point now that having a high income is no guarantee of avoiding financial stress or indebtedness.)

Some have found themselves on their own, either through divorce or death, and are discovering that they now have to sort out their finances by themselves, without any prior experience. Some have immediate challenges with ageing parents, while for others this is a future prospect. Some have health challenges of their own. Some want to retire sooner than others. And of course, people's priorities in life vary widely.

People in the sandwich generation share:

- worries about the prospect of change, of moving from one phase of life into another and dealing with the uncertainty that change brings

- concerns about not knowing where to turn for help

- worries about how they can best guide their young adults towards a sound financial future, especially in an era when finding a permanent, stable job seems rare—and the prospect of young adults buying their own home has become almost an impossibility

- concerns about how they can help their parents deal with getting older, getting their affairs in order and potentially making some tough decisions in the not-too-distant future. How will they deal with having to make decisions about aged care, including the complicated financing involved, if it comes to that?

On the flip side, many in the sandwich generation are enjoying a period of time in which they get to spend more time with their young adult children who have stayed home while they try to save for a deposit for their own home or for travel, possibly while they complete their tertiary education.

People in the sandwich generation are also seeing the benefits of their parents living longer, and with a much higher quality of life, even if that raises new concerns about ensuring that their money lasts as long as possible.

And, of course, many in the sandwich generation wonder how they can prepare themselves for life after work, both psychologically and financially.

This is not just about money. Members of the sandwich generation are on the cusp of a whole new phase of life: a phase that, provided they are properly prepared, should be incredibly positive and enjoyable.

The 'One Day' myth

When people like Andrew and Rebecca come to see me for the first time, most of them are sitting 'close to the line' financially.

This couple are living comfortably by spending most or all of what they earn. Their only major assets are their house and super, and their mortgage is their only major debt. Nevertheless, in reality they are only one large, unexpected expense away from getting into trouble. It could be the discovery of a structural issue with their house, or a sudden health scare.

Whatever it is, an expense of even $10000 or $20000 could be enough to put them into debt, either by having to take out a personal loan or maxing out a credit card. Many people are aware of this vulnerability, but they'd prefer to hope it doesn't happen than face the potential consequences.

Others are already less than comfortable. Some are only just meeting their high mortgage payments every month. While they intend to pay off the credit card in full every month, they often fail to do so. Over time this has seen their credit card debt, and the cost of interest, creep up to the point where it is an ongoing burden. They're getting by, but worrying about money is something they spend a lot of time doing.

Talking to people, whether singles or couples, in either of these situations tends to take a familiar path.

First, they tell me that they've been meaning to get around to organising their finances … for years.

Second, they tell me that they always thought their money challenges would be solved when they got that next promotion, or the better job with a better salary, or even just paying off the mortgage. In other words, they thought it would all be okay 'one day'.

This is what I call the 'One Day' myth.

The 'One Day' myth is the idea that while we might be living on the financial edge now, it will all come together … one day. The money will look after itself … when they have access to a bit more of it.

Sadly, I call this a myth for good reason: it is a myth.

What actually happens, 99 per cent of the time, is that if and when 'a bit more money' comes along—let's say through a pay rise—it is quickly absorbed into an improved lifestyle. A bit more is spent eating out, holidaying in a slightly better hotel, buying a bigger television (either on the credit card or by taking out an 'interest-free' loan) or through any of the myriad other options for spending more money that we are surrounded by.

Why does this happen? For multiple reasons. Most of us like spending money, and having more of it only makes spending all the more tempting. 'I deserve it' is a common refrain, reinforced by marketing everywhere we look.

The other significant factor—perhaps the major one—is that most people don't know where they are spending their money in the first place, so they don't even notice that they have 'adjusted' to spending more now that more is coming in.

Whatever the reason, the point is that you mislead yourself by thinking that your money challenges, small or large, are going to disappear when you get that next pay rise or the better job. It would be far better to get control of your money now and start making meaningful plans for the future.

Reality hits home

The motivation for people like Andrew and Rebecca to come to see someone like me is usually a combination of all the factors I've just described:

- An epiphany that time is moving on: the kids are older, the parents are older…and so are we. 'Life after work' is potentially not as far away as we thought.

- The realisation that the money situation has never really changed despite pay rises in the past, or paying off the mortgage, or a bit of extra money from some other source.

- Suddenly realising that we have no idea where the money is going.

- A creeping awareness that our level of debt has become bigger than we thought, and we're not sure how to deal with it.

- The penny dropping that finally getting the finances in order isn't going to happen without some external help.

It's when one or more of these realisations hits that, hopefully, Andrew and/or Rebecca finally start asking their friends if they can recommend someone who can help.

It's never too late

If you've read this far and you're thinking something like, 'But I'm over 50. Isn't it a bit late to start saving (or investing, or paying down debt) now?', you're not alone. This is something else I hear a lot.

The truth is, it's never too late.

'How can you say that? I always wanted to retire on $100 000 a year from the time I was 60. And now I'm 55 and nowhere near that goal.'

It may well be that meeting that specific goal is not possible. However, it could be feasible to get closer to it with a few adjustments.

First, it's never too late to take control of your money. What's happened in the past can't be changed, but you can definitely change the future and improve things from where they are now. You can take a good look at how you're spending your money now—where the money's going. There will be surprises—there always are—and there will be opportunities to make adjustments. You can also look at your debts and for opportunities to consolidate them, pay them off more quickly or reduce their cost. (All of these will be discussed in more detail later in this book.)

Second, it's probably time for a fresh think about what retirement might look like, and whether or not you have to draw a hard line in the sand at any particular age. Perhaps you can get your superannuation and/or savings to last longer by working part-time for longer—perhaps even in an entirely different sort of work. In my experience, a lot of people who retire at 60 or 65 find themselves getting bored quite quickly. There are only so many games of golf you can play or walks along the beach you can do.

Taking control of your money and rethinking retirement are both ways of revealing for you the most important thing you need right now: options. There won't be any one way forward, and there certainly isn't one way forward that will suit everyone. But options can really open things up for you.

My hope with this book is that it will give you a good start in understanding your current financial and money matters, and some ideas about where you can go from here. It should also give you some insight into how an adviser may be able to help you even further, and how you can go about finding and working with an adviser if you wish to consider that in the future.

PART 1
Back to basics

1

Taking control of your money

What's in this chapter

Control comes from knowledge

Where did the money go?

Take control

Staying in control

Stay informed: Podcasts and books

The way we manage money in our daily lives today is quite different to what was common practice 40-or-so years ago, when those of us in the sandwich generation were still children or young adults. It is unrecognisable from a generation before that.

Once upon a time, the Australian economy ran almost entirely on cash. Cheques could be used to pay some bills, but otherwise if you wanted to spend money, you needed cash in your wallet. Most people were paid in cash—you may remember the common yellow pay packets—and that money had to last. If you were paid into your bank account and needed money for the weekend, you needed to get to the bank before it closed at four o'clock on a Friday afternoon. If you missed it, you were in for a dry weekend.

Two big changes took place in the decade from the mid-1970s.

One of these was the arrival of ATMs, which quickly grew in number from 1980. At last, if we had money in our bank account we could access it at any time—or at least between 7 am and 11 pm, which were the 'working hours' of the early ATMs. A related innovation was EFTPOS, which arrived in the mid-1980s. With EFTPOS, we could access the money in our bank accounts at the checkout.

Since then, the range of products designed to help us 'manage' our money has continued to grow: numerous bank account options, tap-and-go payments, credit cards, instant loan offers, buy-now-pay-later services, mortgage options, superannuation, managed investment funds…the list never ends.

Nevertheless, the principles at the heart of money management remain the same.

If you earn more than you spend, you'll save money over time. If you spend more than you earn, you'll eventually go into debt.

It follows that to have control of your finances you need to know two things: first, how much you are earning; and second, where your money is going (that is, what you're spending it on).

Most people have a reasonable idea of what they earn, but in my experience very few have a good idea of where their money is going. It doesn't matter how old they are or how high their salaries are. It doesn't matter whether they are living very comfortably, living from one payday to the next or struggling with debt. It's nearly always the same. The money is spent but they don't know what it's spent on, or why it always seems to run out at the end of the fortnight or month.

So this is where I start with my clients, and this is where you need to start too.

4

Whether you want to get control of your money to manage your way out of debt or you want to plan for the future (or both), you need to know where the money is going.

When you know that, you'll be in a much better position to take control of your finances.

In this chapter, we will focus on these two things: understanding where the money is going, and taking control of your spending—two essential skills that need to be mastered on the way towards achieving your financial goals.

The big points: Getting control

What you can do right now, no questions asked

1. Compile your bank and credit card statements (paper or online) in preparation for a simple review of your expenditure as described in the upcoming section 'Start here: Work out where it went'.

2. Review your current bank accounts. What accounts do you have, and are you paying any monthly or transaction fees?

3. Familiarise yourself with your current credit card debt. If I said you had to pay all that debt off over the next 10 months, could you comfortably do so?

Control comes from knowledge

The overall theme of this chapter is that 'knowledge is power'. Gaining and maintaining control of your finances starts with knowing where the money is going. The main steps are:

- knowing how you're spending your money now, and checking whether you're spending more or less than you earn

- establishing a simple system for managing your money that will make sure the essential bills are paid while giving you the freedom to have some discretion over how you spend the rest

- maintaining that system by tracking your expenses in an easy way that won't become a chore.

Where did the money go?

Gaining an understanding of where your money is going allows you to make informed choices about what you want to do with what you earn.

For some, this may be a recognition that they don't want to cut back anywhere, which is fine…as long as they can afford that choice and understand the future consequences. They can continue to enjoy their current lifestyle with the added comfort of knowing why their bank balance is never getting any higher.

For others, it will provide areas of focus. If you are surprised by exactly how much you are spending on eating out or buying shoes, you can make choices about reducing that spending. If you find yourself spending more than you earn in every pay period, understanding where the money is going will help you make decisions about where you would prefer to cut back.

I want to reiterate that how much you earn is not the important factor here.

I've known people earning a million dollars a year who spend what they earn every month and have no idea what they're spending it on.

In contrast, I've also known people earning $70 000 a year who have full control of their money, have their first investment property and are well on their way to buying a second. If you know where your money's going, you can make choices about what you do with it—regardless of how much money you are earning.

Start here: Work out where it went

Working out how you are spending your money is a lot easier today than it used to be. Most of us do the majority of our shopping using EFTPOS, either on a direct debit card or a credit card. That means we have a record of what we've spent that appears on the monthly statement for that card. This is obviously a big change from when we used cash for most spending and had to be quite diligent about record keeping if we wanted to track our expenditure.

A simple review of expenditure

Here's what a review of your recent expenditure might look like:

1. **Dig out (or download) the last three to 12 months of your bank account and credit card statements.** Ideally, this expenditure review will cover a full 12 months in order to capture any large one-off items such as car insurance, but we find that three months is usually enough to reveal a few surprises about where the money is going.

2. **For these statements, tally up your expenditure by category, such as groceries, car, eating out/takeaways, rent or mortgage, electricity, gas, and so on.** How broad or narrow your categories are isn't so important at this stage—you're just trying to get a better idea of how you're spending your money. Your bank's online banking facility may be able to help you with this task. Many banks now provide a basic automatic categorisation of expenses. If this is the case with your bank, you may need to check that the categorisation is accurate, but it can be a starting point.

3. **Review what the numbers are telling you—the (perhaps harsh) reality of where you are spending your money.**

This exercise is almost always a revelation. It is guaranteed to prompt comments like, 'I never realised how much we spend on takeaways!' or 'How am I spending that much on coffee?'

But this revelation is also an opportunity: an opportunity to immediately modify your spending habits and take control of your money.

Relax! I'm not going to ask you to create a budget

Notice that I'm not using the word 'budget' in this chapter. If you are in your 50s or later, I'm betting you were taught at some stage that controlling money is all about budgeting: taking your monthly income and dividing it up among various expense categories, then ensuring that what you spend in each category is within the assigned limit.

Budgeting like this is great in theory, but I have found it doesn't work very well in practice for most people. That's why hardly anyone does it. It's too much hard work.

Budgeting is a bit like dieting in that it has negative connotations. Like dieting, living on a budget implies missing out on the fun stuff. (It doesn't—I can assure you of that from personal experience, but it's hard to overcome the perception.) What's more, if you've reached your 50s without budgeting, I can almost guarantee that you're not going to start now, no matter how much I or anyone else encourages you to.

Knowing where your money is going and simply using that knowledge to take control by better managing your cash flow is usually a lot easier, and therefore more successful, than strict budgeting.

Take control

Once you know where your money is going, you're in a good position to take control of it. By following a few simple steps, including possibly adding a new bank account, you'll soon be in charge. If it's a long time since you've had such control, you'll be amazed at how good it feels.

I'm going to outline the steps briefly first, which may be enough to get you started.

1. Sort

The first step is to sort your current expenses out into those that are 'essential' versus 'discretionary', and those that are 'regular' (or routine) versus 'day-to-day'. By the end of this step, each expense will have two labels: essential or discretionary, and regular or day-to-day.

Essential or discretionary?

For each expense category you created in 'A simple review of expenditure', label it as either 'essential' or 'discretionary'.

An *essential* expense is fairly self-explanatory. It's spending on something that you need to live. In some cases it will be an expense that will have unpleasant consequences if you don't pay it, such as losing your home or having the power cut off. Common examples are mortgage or rent payments, utility bills (such as water, electricity and your internet connection), insurance premiums, and car registration. Other essential categories would usually include groceries, petrol and/ or public transport, medications, and so on.

We can loosely define *discretionary* expenses as 'nice to haves', optional or not strictly essential. Some might call these luxuries, though that gets tricky because many people—myself included—won't regard their daily coffee as a luxury. Common discretionary categories would typically include eating out/takeaways, movies and theatre, clothes (beyond the basics), gym membership, subscriptions to television streaming services like Netflix, or a wine subscription service.

Regular or day-to-day?

Your next task is to go through your list of categories again, this time labelling each as either 'regular' or 'day-to-day'.

Regular expenses are those that come out of your bank account in a routine manner, or that you pay in response to receiving a bill. There's a good chance you pay most regular expenses through your internet banking service, either through an automatic direct debit arrangement with the provider or using BPAY.

In contrast, *day-to-day* expenses are those that you pay for when you're out and about, either using cash or EFTPOS (on a debit or credit card). Increasingly, people are using 'tap-and-go' services for these payments. You might pay cash for your coffee, while using EFTPOS at the supermarket, bottle shop and service station. For most people, most of their discretionary spending will fall under the 'day-to-day' heading.

Once you've put each category into either the regular or day-to-day 'bucket', go through and add both groups up to create a total for regular expenses and a total for day-to-day expenses. Finally, divide each of these numbers by the number of pay periods it represents to give you an average total per pay period.

Here's an example based on the monthly average family spend in 2015–16[1] (this Spending Analysis template is available at themoneysandwich.com):

---

[1] Australian Bureau of Statistics. Household Expenditure Survey, 2015–16.

SIMPLIFIED SPENDING ANALYSIS EXAMPLE

(Totals per month; based on a salary of $100 000
= after tax $6292 per month)

	Regular (paid from Savings Account)		Day-to-day (paid from Everyday Account)	
Essential	Mortgage	$1600	Petrol	$350
	Electricity/gas	$300	Groceries	$900
	Car rego/insurance	$600	Chemist	$100
	Medical	$300	Public transport	$200
	Credit card	$200	Clothes (basics)	$200
Discretionary	Streaming TV	$70	Movies/shows	$100
	Paper/books	$70	Taxis	$150
	Gym	$100	Takeaway	$300
	Holidays/saving	$250	Fashion	$500
	'Regular' = $3490		**'Day-to-day' = $2800**	

Total = $6290
(Total should be lower than your monthly income)

Average family spend in 2016 was $6191.75 per month

Our end goal here is to be able to separate each incoming salary payment into two parts: 'regular' and 'day-to-day' (each of these parts are further divided into 'essential' and 'discretionary'). The example does this assuming a monthly pay packet.

Our next step will be to 'physically' separate our regular and day-to-day funds into separate bank accounts.

2. Bank and spend

Most people live pay packet to pay packet.

This may be a hangover from the old days when we were provided a physical pay packet of cash at the end of every week. Now, of course, almost everyone is paid by electronic transfer (to be paid cash today would feel decidedly questionable). And you receive your pay at best fortnightly, often monthly.

On one hand, we've lost physical touch with our money—now it's just a number in our banking app rather than a wad of notes. On the other, we need to be better at managing each pay—especially those who are paid monthly.

What I see is a lot of people who live very well for the first two weeks of the month, not so great in the third week as the bank account starts to look a bit light, and then really struggle in that fourth week while they hang out for the next pay to come through. It's in this week that there is the real temptation to use credit cards or easy payday loans to fill the gap. By the end of the month there's nothing left, and definitely not enough to put towards building a savings nest egg.

A system for managing your cash flow

Businesses get good at managing their cash flow: matching what they spend and when they spend it against what they earn and when they earn it.

There's no reason why we can't do something very similar with our home accounts. In fact, most of us can do this much more easily than a business because we know exactly what we're going to earn before we earn it. Most businesses don't have that luxury.

The bank-and-spend system I want to suggest provides a way of recreating that weekly pay packet feeling, which makes managing your money from one week to the next, and between paydays, a whole lot easier.

This works at any age, so if it works for you, please share it with your adult children as well.

Here's how it works.

At its most basic, you need to have two separate but linked bank accounts: an 'everyday' transaction account and a 'savings' account.

The savings account is where your salary is paid into, and that account can then provide a weekly 'personal wage' to your everyday account. This helps smooth out your income across each pay period.

It's a very simple concept, but most people who try it find that just knowing they have to make the money last until the end of the week makes controlling their finances a lot easier.

Everyday account — your personal expense account

You can think of your 'everyday' account as your personal expense account.

You use the debit card attached to your everyday account to pay for goods and services when you're out and about—what we called 'day-to-day' expenses in step 1, where we sorted your expenses into regular or day-to-day expenses.

Savings account — your operations account

Your 'savings' account serves two purposes. It is the account into which your salary is paid. You can also use this account to pay the 'regular' expenses described in step 1, in most cases via online banking (such as BPAY). You might think of this account as your 'operations account'—sort of like the business account for your home finances. It's for keeping the lights on.

Using the two accounts together

An effective way to use these accounts together is like this:

1. **Your pay goes into your savings account.**

2. **You then pay yourself a 'personal wage' by transferring one week's worth of day-to-day expenses into your everyday account—your personal expense account.** Accessing your everyday funds with your debit card, you pay for all day-to-day expenses out of that account, up to a maximum of the weekly transfer.

   Remember, if these funds run out, you'll have to tighten your belt until your next 'personal wage' payment is made, so you need to keep your eye on this account's balance.

3. **During the week you pay bills for regular expenses out of your savings account—in other words, your operations account.**

4. **At the end of the week, you top up your personal expense account by transferring another week's worth of day-to-day expenses from your savings account to your everyday account.** A good option would be to set up this transfer to happen automatically.

The following flow chart shows this flow of salary income:

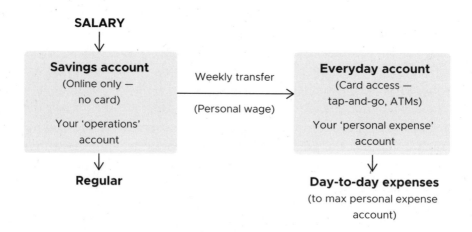

Banking products: Shop around for the best deal

Competition between banks has become very tight in recent years, which can only be a good thing for those who want to use their services. So, if you're going to rearrange some of your banking to suit the system I'm proposing here, this might also be a good time to check what fees, if any, you are currently being charged to operate your existing accounts.

You really shouldn't be paying any fees at all for things like account keeping, ATM withdrawals or excess EFTPOS transactions. If you find you are still paying account-related fees, it might be time to shop around for an alternative bank.

Perhaps you should shop around anyway. Most people still have all their loans, credit cards, savings accounts, and so on with the one bank — the 'one-stop shop' approach — however, this is certainly not necessary. It would be rare that a single bank is able to offer the best deal in all areas. While banks have introduced more and more technology as a way of reducing their costs, we can use that technology to help us find the best deals: the most attractive loan options (low interest and low fees), fee-free bank accounts, low-fee credit cards with longer interest-free periods, high-interest savings accounts, and so on. Internet banking makes moving money between accounts at different banks very simple — and usually instant — these days. You could find yourself saving thousands in fees and earning much more from your savings.

If it's cheaper to have your mortgage with one bank, your transaction accounts with another and a high-interest account with another, that's worth considering.

---

3. Review

If you successfully take control of your spending along the lines I've just described, you will probably be surprised how quickly you gain even more clarity about your spending habits.

After just two or three pay periods, you'll be getting a good sense of whether your weekly 'personal wage' is more or less than you find comfortable. As in so many situations, it is best to keep your new system as simple as possible in the beginning, say for the next six months or so. However, there are some easy adjustments that can be made to 'tweak' your new situation. This is where that control you have over your money really comes into its own.

Here are a few common situations you may experience in the first few weeks.

I'm running short in my personal expense account

This is not unusual in the early stages, so it's important not to see falling short in your everyday account as a sign of failure. Rather, it is a sign that your numbers need adjusting.

Put simply, you have two choices in this situation: you can increase your personal wage, or you can reduce your day-to-day spending.

The beauty of using a separate account for your day-to-day spending is that already, by separating out your regular bills, you will probably have a better sense of where you are spending your money day-to-day. This should make opportunities to reduce your spending fairly easy to identify without having to get into sophisticated analysis.

Can you reduce eating out by one meal a week? Can you prepare lunch at home two or three days a week rather than buying it? Small things can make a difference.

Alternatively, you can increase your weekly personal wage to cover your higher-than-expected day-to-day expenses—provided you won't leave your savings account short for the payment of important bills.

If you take this path, my suggestion is to make small adjustments rather than large ones. Add say 5 per cent to your weekly personal expenses and see whether you can manage with that increased amount for a couple of weeks.

Remember: there are no absolute rules here. It's your money, and you have control over it. What we are trying to do here is give you that control so that you can make your own decisions.

My total spending exceeds my salary

Again, discovering that your total spending is in excess of your salary is not a sign of failure. Having this knowledge is an important step forward. Nevertheless, with the reality of the situation now laid out in front of you, it's time to think about where you can cut back.

This might be a good time to revisit the analysis you did back in step 1 (the 'sort' step). Start by targeting the larger expenses—both regular and day-to-day—and look for opportunities to reduce your costs. I can't give you absolute guidance here because everyone's situation will be different, but this process might give you the impetus to shop around for a better deal on your power bills, your internet connection, your home and car insurance, and so on.

Companies offering general insurance, such as car insurance or home and contents insurance—life insurance is different—often rely on what is sometimes called a 'lazy tax', lifting premiums year after year on the assumption that their customers won't bother shopping around. A quick online comparison for these types of insurance might find you some instant savings.

Other potential savings might be found in smaller expenses: the number of television or music streaming services you are subscribed to; other subscriptions, such as to newspapers and magazines; and so on.

There will always be ways to reduce spending without changing your lifestyle too much…once you know where your money is going each month.

I want to be proactive about saving

You might find yourself in the happy (and preferred) position of having enough in your day-to-day account to meet your needs (with all your regular expenses paid), and still having some money left in your savings account at the end of the month or pay period.

Obviously, this is the ideal situation to be in. Now, because you have your money under control, you are able to make proactive decisions about what to do with your surplus funds.

You could increase the amount you pay into your personal expense account and 'live it up' a bit. You could leave those funds in your savings account and watch them grow, knowing that they're there to help you out should something unforeseen happen (or a bill arrive that you weren't expecting).

Ideally, you will open a separate high-interest savings account in which to build your savings over time.

The third bank account: High-interest savings

A separate high-interest savings account or term deposit account can be used to 'lock away' and build your savings where you won't be tempted to touch them. The idea is that they stay there until you reach a specific savings goal (for example, buying a car or putting a deposit on a house), reinvest the funds into another investment (such as shares or property) or need to draw on them for some sort of emergency. This account does not need to be with the same bank as your other accounts—you want the account that is offering the highest rate of interest.

This is the approach we find ourselves recommending to many of our clients to help them stay on track to meet their longer-term goals.

A good approach is to treat your monthly savings amount like any other regular payment. You set up an automatic transfer so that each month, after your salary goes into your savings account, your savings amount is transferred into the high-interest account. In this way, if you get to the end of the month and have nothing left in your savings and everyday accounts for whatever reason, at least you have already put aside those savings. They are already earning higher interest for you. A regular, disciplined savings regime like this is the easiest and best way to build up your savings over time in your goals account.

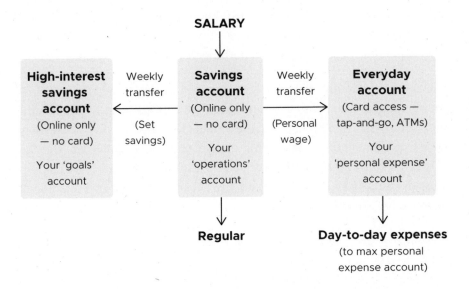

At the moment, I like the way Macquarie Bank provides linked accounts that can serve all three purposes: savings, everyday and high interest (macquarie.com.au/everyday-banking). The ING Direct Savings Maximiser (ing.com.au/savings) and Citibank Online Saver (citibank.com.au/banking) are other popular options with higher interest that are easy to use and can be linked. For those who want to save without thinking, Raiz (raizinvest.com.au) and Spaceship Voyager (spaceship.com.au/voyager) work well as apps for your spare change. In addition, the Canstar website (canstar.com.au) provides tools for comparing current options.

I'm having trouble deciding whether some expenses are essential or discretionary

There will always be some expense categories that sit on the border between essential and discretionary. Unfortunately, there are rarely any absolute answers on this: only you can decide where to draw your line between what you need and what is nice to have.

One way to think about it is to consider how easy it would be to reduce or postpone spending in a given category. Reducing your mortgage, for instance, is not something that can be done easily, or that you would do very often. While there are ways to reduce your power bills (including shopping around and being more efficient with power use—both recommended), again, it isn't something you'll do every month.

On the other hand, everyone has options about how many coffees they buy, how often they eat out and at what price level of restaurant, how often they get home-delivered food, whether to buy those new shoes or that leather jacket this month or wait a while, whether to subscribe to three streaming services at a time or just one, and so on. Most discretionary expenses, then, are those that could be pulled back or put off at short notice.

Even if your new money management system works well right from the start, it's a good idea to review your situation regularly in the short term and longer term. In this way, you'll maintain control and continue to be in a position to make positive, proactive decisions about what you do with your money.

What if I can't get control?

If even after working out how much you are spending you realise there is no more to cut and you are going to continue to build up debt, it's important to know there are places you can go to get assistance. Don't just ignore the situation. Some contact numbers are listed in Chapter 10 if you need to know who to call.

A lesson of the COVID-19 experience

If I ever needed assurance that Australians need more education about money, and in particular getting control of it, it was during the COVID-19 pandemic in 2020. If media reports are anything to go by, there were a very large number of people who entered the crisis with savings equivalent to less than one month's expenditure. This was reinforced by the number of people who found themselves needing early access to their superannuation savings after the federal government made that option available. Over 3.4 million people applied for this 'Early Release Scheme' benefit, with around a million twice, and $36 billion was withdrawn as of the end of December 2020 (Australian Prudential Regulatory Authority).

Having a minimum of three months' salary available—in a readily accessible bank account, via a drawdown facility against your mortgage, for example—is one of the basics of any good financial plan. If you don't have that now, I recommend it as a priority to work towards as soon as you can.

Staying in control

As you settle into your new level of control over your money, you may find that you would like to find ways to track your finances on an ongoing basis so that you can tweak things like your personal wage or set up and monitor a savings plan.

We are fortunate today to have a number of tools available to us to assist with this task. Depending on how deeply you want to get into this, and how much of your own effort you want to put into it, you have three main options to choose from:

- **Bank-based analysis.** Your bank may already provide, via its internet banking facility, some categorisation of your spending. This may be fairly simple and you probably can't modify the categories, but it would be a good start. The main disadvantage with bank-based analysis is if you have bank accounts or credit cards with more than one bank, in which case one bank's analysis will only provide part of the picture.

- **Apps and online tools.** An increasing number of online and app-based money management tools are available, some free and some charging a small monthly fee. These can be set up to automatically import your transaction data from all your banks, and then categorise that data for you, removing most of the hassle of tracking your expenses manually. Most of these allow some customisation of the categories and the way they categorise, allowing for a more accurate picture of where your money is going. One I have used with my clients is myprosperity[2] (available through financial advisers), which includes property valuations. A free option available to anyone is Pocketbook (getpocketbook.com) and there are many others out there to choose from.

- **Professional financial advice.** You can organise with your financial adviser or wealth coach to monitor your finances on your behalf, checking in every two or three months to discuss how things have been progressing, what your current goals are and what changes, if any, you might want to make. Like a personal trainer, your adviser can keep you honest and on track, particularly if this is not a personal strength or if you just don't enjoy the administrative side of managing your money.

Whichever approach you choose to take, it is important to maintain some level of control of your money into the future. You've made great inroads by this point, so it would be a pity to slip back into old habits and have to start all over again.

Maintaining control is also important if you want to manage debt, investment and retirement planning as we will discuss in the next few chapters of this book.

Stay informed: Podcasts and books

Listening to podcasts and reading books on money matters are a great way to build your knowledge base, especially for young adults. I recommend a few popular options here.

---

[2] I will only recommend products that I have used for myself or my own clients. You should do your own research or seek professional advice.

Podcasts:

- **My Millennial Money**—Glen James and John Pidgeon

- **She's on the Money**—Victoria Devine

- **Talking Money with the Nerds**—Fraser Jack and Erin Truscott

- **SBS On the Money**—Ricardo Gonçalves

- **The Good Money Habits**—Julia Schortinghuis

- **The Grass is Greener**—Tim Henry

- **Your Money Story**—Dawn Thomas

- **Money Madams**—Katherine Hayes and Amber Parr

Books:

- **The Joy of Money**—Kate McCallum and Julia Newbould

- **Wonder Woman's Guide to Money**—Natasha Janssens

- **Financial Secrets Revealed**—Amanda Cassar

- **Don't Panic Aged Care Survival Guide**—Louise Biti and Nick Bruining

- **Finance Action Hero**—Peita Diamantidis

- **Get Unstuck**—Ben Nash

- **Money magazine**—if you prefer a regular magazine instead!

Your action plan and next steps

☐ Review your cash flow—use the template I share in this chapter to help split your spending into essential or discretionary, and regular or day-to-day.

☐ Set up separate bank accounts to help manage your cash flow.

☐ Start a savings plan—a small monthly amount at first so you won't miss it. Ideally, this will be automatically deducted as your first expense after you are paid your salary.

In Chapter 10, I share a full 12-month action plan incorporating many of these actions. In addition, my website (themoneysandwich.com) has plenty of templates, calculators and general information to help you with this process.

2

Getting to grips with debt

What's in this chapter

Debt considerations

Debts ain't debts: Separating the good from the bad

The big debts

Wrangling bad debt

Prior to 1974, aside from the relatively rare (by today's standards) use of services like hire purchase and personal loans, most people's only significant debt was the mortgage on their house. And that was a big deal. Obtaining a mortgage meant dressing up for a meeting with your bank manager in his wood-panelled office. You needed ample evidence of not only your ability to meet the mortgage payments, but also of your standing as a good citizen.

Otherwise, the vast majority of Australians only spent what they could afford. If they wanted to buy a television, they saved up for it. Likewise furniture. It wasn't unusual for a newly married couple to move into an almost empty home, which they gradually filled with belongings over many years. If there was a product you really wanted but couldn't afford right now, you could put it on lay-by, whereby you paid for it over time and only collected the item once it was fully paid off.

Bankcard, Australia's first credit card, changed all that when it was launched in 1974. Widespread access to Bankcard meant that the average Australian's access to money was no longer restricted to what was in their bank account and pocket. Where previously the idea of borrowing money for everyday spending was foreign to most people, it didn't take long for it to become the new normal. With the help of some heavy marketing, within 18 months over one million Australians—more than 6 per cent of the population at the time—had a Bankcard in their wallet or purse.

A few years ago, I was at a conference and the presenter asked us to cross our arms normally and to notice how natural that felt. He then asked us to cross our arms the other way and to notice how unnatural that felt. He asked us to hold our arms in that unnatural position for a full minute, after which a strange thing happened. It suddenly felt perfectly natural to have our arms crossed in this unusual way. It was fascinating how quickly we adapted—how quickly the abnormal became normal.

This situation is a good analogy for the way Australians have adapted to living in debt. In fact, Australians have become so comfortable with debt that we rank near the top of the world rankings[3] for household debt, with high debt in mortgages, personal loans and credit cards, among others.

In this chapter, we look at the major forms of debt and some strategies for managing them.

---

[3] OECD data, 2015.

The big points: Taking control of debt

What you can do right now, no questions asked

1. Read the upcoming section 'Debts ain't debts: Separating the good from the bad' on the difference between 'good' debt and 'bad' debt. This distinction is critical to taking control of your debt.

2. Review your existing credit card debt, if any. What do you owe, and how long will it take to pay off if you continue your current approach to repayments?

3. Review any existing personal loans, small or large. Be aware of how much interest you are paying. Consider whether you can increase your regular repayments to reduce the term of the loan and save yourself some interest.

4. Review your mortgage if you still have one. How are you tracking to pay it off before you retire?

Debt considerations

Before you take on any debt:

- **Be fully aware of the purpose of the loan.** Are you borrowing for an investment asset that will provide an income, or for a lifestyle asset (for fun)?

- **Borrow based on how much you can afford, not how much the bank is willing to give you.** I always double the current interest rate and check whether I could still afford the loan under those conditions. Interest rates might be low now, but eventually they will go up.

- **Include some flexibility for an unexpected reduction of income.** For instance, if your calculation of your ability to repay a loan is based on your income from two salaries, ask yourself whether you could still afford it if you only had one of those salaries.

- **On mortgages or personal loans, aim to pay back 20 to 30 per cent more than the standard repayments.** All that extra money will come off the principal, and with the benefits of compounding you might reduce the time taken to pay off the loan by as much as half the term.

Debts ain't debts: Separating the good from the bad

Before we get into a discussion about debt management, it's important that we clearly distinguish between 'good' debt and 'bad' debt. This is particularly important for members of the sandwich generation because using good debt to your advantage can be a powerful way of preparing yourself for your post-work phases of life. The key to successful debt management is to use good debt as a tool while minimising the negative effects of bad debt.

Let's define these terms.

Good debt is debt that provides the funds to buy an asset that provides an ongoing income.

Bad debt is pretty much all other debt. Any debt that does not have an income-producing asset behind it—even if it provides capital growth—is bad debt.

Examples of good debt

Good debt allows us to buy good, income-producing assets, the value of which outpaces our ability to save for them.

Say you want to buy a $500 000 investment property today but only have $100 000 to spend. By the time you save the remaining $400 000—let's say it takes you 10 years—the property's value has risen to $1 million. It is even further out of reach. In contrast, if you used your $100 000 as a deposit and borrowed the $400 000, you could buy the property today and take advantage of that capital growth, and the rental income, over the next 10 years.

Borrowing for property investment is a common example of good debt. First, the debt is attached to an asset—the property. If it's a good property it will appreciate in value over time. Second, that property will provide you with a regular income in the form of rent. It's that income stream that is the hidden gem of good debt.

Another example would be borrowing to buy good-quality shares. When you buy shares, you are effectively buying ownership of a part of the company (albeit a very small part in most cases). When the company earns a profit, as most good companies regularly do, they'll pay you, as a shareholder, a proportion of that profit as a dividend, usually every six months. Historically, share prices will go up and down over time, though the market has always gone up overall in the long term. But the price only matters when you're buying and selling. What really matters, again, is that income stream.

You could also borrow to establish your own business which, assuming it is a good business, will provide you with an income. That would be another form of good debt, although the income it generates will of course be dependent on you working on the business and ensuring its profitability.

I discuss each of these examples in more detail in the next chapter. However, I do want to make the point now that in each of these cases, and indeed any case of taking out a substantial loan, it is important that you do your research. You need to have confidence in the underlying value of the asset you are buying and in the amount of income it will realistically generate.

One exception to the rule about debt providing an income is the mortgage on your home. Provided it remains under control and is paid off before you retire, your mortgage can be classified as good debt even though the asset (your home) doesn't provide you with an income. This is a unique case. The main reason is that you do need to live somewhere, and if you're living in your home you're not having to pay rent elsewhere. (It also provides a significant tax advantage in that there's no capital gains tax to pay when you sell it, which I explain in more detail in Chapter 4.)

Examples of bad debt

Borrowing to buy a car has become so common that many take it for granted. This has led to a widespread misconception that a car is an 'investment', and therefore a car loan is an acceptable form of debt. However, while it's true that we nearly all need a car, and that it can be difficult to come up with the cash to buy one outright, a car loan is unquestionably a form of bad debt using my earlier definition. Not only does a car lose substantial value the minute you drive it out of the showroom, and continue to lose value thereafter, it also doesn't provide you with any form of income. On the contrary, running your car is likely to be one of the largest expenses in your monthly budget. Things get even worse if you find yourself using your credit card to pay for, say, a set of new tyres and then paying interest on that debt as well.

Luxury cars are a common form of bad debt for those who earn high incomes. That expensive car is lovely to drive, and you can afford the repayments, so why not? There is no problem with this scenario provided you understand that your choice to drive this fancy car is a lifestyle choice, not an investment. Higher-priced cars depreciate in value more quickly than lower-priced ones, and they typically cost more to run, with notoriously high service costs. My suggestion before investing in a luxury car would be to work out the real weekly price of running your chosen car, including depreciation, interest and running costs, and make sure you are comfortable with that cost before you commit to buying.

Many other lifestyle choices are also examples of bad debt if they require borrowing to make them happen. Perhaps you have a passion for fishing and want to borrow to buy a boat. Or you need a loan for that new set of golf clubs or a high-end road bike. None of these meet the income-producing test hurdle of good debt.

I'm not trying to suggest that lifestyle assets are a bad thing. It's important to enjoy life. However, it's also important to understand the implications of the decisions you make and the true cost of your purchases—the risk versus the reward.

Other examples of bad debt include any form of borrowing to pay for a product or service *right now* because you don't want to wait until payday (or worse, the payday after that) to have the necessary cash. This might apply to clothes, holidays, entertainment, a new television or any other consumer goods. These are typically the items that people pay for using a credit card, an in-store no- or low-interest loan or, increasingly, a buy-now-pay-later service.

There is no problem with using these types of payment facilities for convenience, including to even out your cash flow—*provided* you understand and can afford the associated fees and charges—*and* you avoid paying the associated very high rates of interest by paying your credit card bill or the loan *in full* by the nominated deadline.

The big debts

The major debts held by Australians, in decreasing order, are home mortgages, investment loans, personal loans, student debt (mainly HECS-HELP) and credit card debt.

In this chapter, we look at credit cards, personal loans and home mortgages. In Chapter 4, we look at using debt for investments. I don't discuss student debt in this book, as it is less of an issue for the sandwich generation—especially those lucky enough to have gone to university during the 12 years that it was free. Also, HECS-HELP debt is deducted as a small and manageable part of your adult children's salary once over a certain level and, for most, is interest free so not too much of an issue.

Credit cards: The everyday debt

Since the arrival of that first credit card, the debt culture in Australia has grown at a staggering rate. In 2019,[4] there were over 15.5 million credit cards on issue in Australia with a total balance of $50.5 billion, or just over $3200 owing per card. Around 70 per cent of adult Australians have at least one credit card, with the 35–54-year-old age group having the highest rate of card ownership.

Add newer technologies like tap-and-go, including making payments with a touch of your phone or smart watch, and it has never been easier to spend without thinking. It's all a far cry from carefully managing the contents of your pay packet.

Now, for those people who have control of their money — who know what they're spending and how much they can afford to spend, and who pay their credit cards off monthly so avoid accruing interest — all of this is a convenience rather than a problem. However, there is another group of people for whom easy credit is a real-world, day-to-day challenge. Of that $50.5 billion held in credit card debt in 2019, just over $30 billion was accruing penalty interest, and that debt belonged to only around one-third of credit card holders.

While credit card and related debt can be high among members of the sandwich generation, my experience is that a greater level of stress caused by this type of debt exists among young adults. This is the number-one concern of many of the sandwich generation couples I see, whose children are now in their early 20s. Debt among this age group is fed by slick advertising offering quick and easy loans, and, according to some of our clients, by easy online access to gambling, particularly on sports.

---

[4] Reserve Bank of Australia data, 2019.

One final point to make here is that credit card and similar debt is not only a problem for those on lower incomes. In my experience, a higher income often means a higher level of lifestyle, and typically a higher level of debt goes along with that.

Now, none of this is to suggest that we should wind the clock back to the way things were in 1960. Debt is a reality of our age and that isn't going to change. We need to acknowledge that there are some forms of debt — 'good debt' — that you can use to your benefit. We look at both good and bad debt in the rest of this chapter.

Credit card home truths

The hidden costs of credit cards are often misunderstood. Let's look at two common scenarios.

Jen used a credit card to buy a lounge suite for $2000. She made no other purchases on that card. When her next bill arrived, it showed a 'minimum payment' of $41 per month, which she assumed was all she had to pay.

Unfortunately, Jen was overlooking the exceptionally high (but typical of credit cards) interest rate of 20 per cent per annum that applied to her remaining balance. That had the potential to be a very expensive oversight. Assuming Jen continued to pay just the minimum balance on that card, it would have taken her just under 25 years to pay off the card, by which time the lounge suite was likely long gone. Over the period, she would have paid over $5700 in interest, meaning her $2000 sofa actually cost her $7700.

Luckily Jen noticed the fine print on her credit card bill that detailed these numbers. The bill also showed that if she paid off $100 per month instead of $41, she would have paid off the card in total in two years, with a total interest cost of $403. That's still quite a lot of interest, but a lot less than nearly $6000.

(continued)

Declan was in a different situation. He used his credit card primarily for the convenience. By putting most of his day-to-day expenses on his card, then paying off the monthly bill in full before the due date, he paid no interest on his card balance. This kept his average bank balance higher which, via an offset, kept his mortgage balance and the associated interest cost down. As a bonus, he accrued a few frequent flyer points along the way.

This system worked well until one month when Declan forgot to pay off a $3000 card account by the due date. By the time he realised his mistake only a couple of days later, that 20 per cent per annum interest was already accruing on his account balance of $5000—the $3000 on that latest statement plus the $2000 he had spent since that statement was issued. His account would continue to accrue interest until that entire balance had been paid off. Luckily for Declan he was able to access the cash required to immediately transfer $5000 to his credit card account, thus stopping the interest 'clock'. However, he still ended up having around $100 in interest added to his next bill. It was an expensive oversight, and one that would have been even more expensive the longer he had let it go.

How to keep credit card debt under control

People typically use credit cards in one of two ways: by paying them off *in full* every month, or by paying off *part* of their credit card debt every month (while trying not to increase it any further). The way you incorporate credit cards into the banking and spending system I outlined in Chapter 1 will depend on which of these two ways of using credit cards applies to you.

A third group of credit card users are those who maintain a card only for occasional convenience, rather than as a cash flow tool. These users also tend to pay off their card in full each month. (If this is you, make sure you are using a fee-free card.)

I pay off my credit card in full every month

If you use your credit card(s) primarily for the convenience, and/or to offset your mortgage, paying the card off completely every month, then you can use the card as another way of accessing your personal expense account.

The trick is making sure the total of what you spend on the credit card *plus* what you spend using your everyday account debit card is no more than your weekly personal wage.

I have a credit card debt and pay part of that debt off every month

There are three rules of thumb I like to apply to credit card debts:

- **Your total credit card debt should be no more than what you can afford to pay off over 10 months; that is, over 10 monthly payments.** In other words, don't let your credit card debt get any larger than you can afford to pay off over the next 10 months as a maximum. If your balance ever gets beyond that point, you should stop using that card until you can bring it back under control (that is, you can pay it off over 10 months). Ignore the limit the credit card company has given you: they are encouraging you to spend more so that you'll have more interest to pay. There is a reason these companies make so much profit.

- **Your monthly payment should be included as a regular payment in your spending plan (as described in Chapter 1), to be paid out of your savings account.**

- **Your monthly payment should equal at least 10 per cent of the total bill for that month.**

What if I'm starting this system with my credit card balance already too large?

If you're starting out with a credit card bill that is already higher than you'll be able to pay off over the next 10 months, your first step is to bring that card back under control.

1. **Put the card away (and delete it from your phone if you're using Google Pay or Apple Pay).** (Some banks allow you to switch cards on and off, which might be a second level of protection against using the card during this period.)

2. **Work out what you can afford to pay off as a regular expense and make that payment religiously.**

3. **If you have more than one card, pay off the one with the highest interest rate first.**

4. **Don't bring the card back out until its balance is comfortably back under the 10-month limit.**

Do I really need a credit card?

There is a third option beyond paying off your card in full or in part each month, which is, of course, to have no credit cards at all. This is a good option in terms of staying out of debt, but it's not always realistic. In reality most people do have one or two credit cards, even if they don't use them often. There are times when they are necessary, such as when making car hire reservations or booking into a hotel, for instance. Debit cards attached to your everyday account are a good alternative in many, if not most, situations as they give you access to the enormous Visa and Mastercard networks. But even the best savers sometimes still need to use a credit card at some point or other. Keeping your card(s) under control (or getting control of them), just like the rest of your spending, is what you're aiming for.

How to best use your credit card

Peter and Jon each owe $3000 on their credit cards.

Peter, using the 10-month rule of thumb, knows he can afford this level of debt because he has $300 left in his savings account each month, and so uses that money to pay down his credit card.

At the end of 10 months, assuming no additional spending, he will have around $200 left on the card — the interest accrued over the 10-month period.

In contrast, Jon has just enough left in his savings account to make the minimum repayment specified on his monthly credit card statement. At $61 each month, this is only a little more than the interest payable. If he continued to pay off the card this way, it would take Jon over 25 years to pay off the credit card, even with no more spending from now on. In that time he would have paid the bank $9251 in total, of which over $6000 would have been interest.

Note that in these examples we're assuming that neither Peter nor Jon uses his credit card for any additional purchases over the periods involved.

Interest of $200 compared to $6000 makes this rule of thumb so worthwhile. Luckily Peter gave Jon the heads up and while he could not pay $300 back each month, he could afford $150 (and put the credit card away). This brought the 25-year repayment period down to just over two years, which still represents a sizeable interest saving.

Personal loans

Credit cards are by no means the only form of debt that is heavily marketed at us. Personal loans feature heavily as well, and they come in a dazzling array of forms, and in fact make up a greater proportion of the debt owed by Australians than credit card debt.

Aside from the 'traditional' financing offers available for large items like cars, there are 'interest-free periods' offered by department stores and a growing number of buy-now-pay-later products. It's not hard to see how Australians, like the populations of most other developed nations, have become addicted to having now what they can only (possibly) afford to pay for later.

Types of personal loan

There are two main types of personal loan, based on the nature of the interest charged and whether or not the loan is secured. In addition, payday loans and 'buy-now-pay-later' financing are two other ways you can be loaned money for personal use.

Variable interest loans versus fixed interest loans

A *variable interest loan* is one in which your bank or other lender can vary the applicable interest rate over time. In contrast, the interest rate on a fixed interest loan is set for the term of the loan.

Fixed interest loans often suit those who feel better knowing exactly what their monthly repayments will be over the life of the loan. Variable interest loans are usually preferred by those who wish to pay off the loan sooner, as any fees associated with early repayment are usually lower.

Secured loans versus unsecured loans

A *secured loan* is a loan on which you have provided some form of 'collateral'; in other words, it is backed by an asset (such as the car you are borrowing the money for). If you fail to repay the loan, your lender will be able to repossess this asset to get their money back.

Unsecured loans are not supported by such an asset, so they expose the lender to a higher level of risk. In some cases a lender may require a guarantor for an unsecured loan. The guarantor becomes legally responsible for repayments if you fail to make them yourself.

Secured loans are generally associated with lower interest rates because of the lower level of risk to the lender.

Payday loans

Payday loans—sometimes disguised under other terms such as 'cash advance' or 'small personal loans'—are a type of 'instant' loan whereby the lender offers to lend a relatively small amount of money (generally up to $2000) for a short term (for example, until your next payday).

These are unsecured loans that appear quick and easy. Often they have smart-looking apps, offer payment within minutes and claim to be interest free. However, they are usually associated with very high fees that can quickly mount up to much more than the original loan amount. For instance, a $2000 payday loan held over 12 months would cost around $3400 in overall repayments.

Remember, payday loans should be avoided under all circumstances.

Nil-interest loans (NIL), low-interest loans and Centrelink advance payments are all alternatives. Check the Australian Securities and Investments Commission's (ASIC's) Moneysmart website for options.

Buy-now-pay-later financing

Buy-now-pay-later arrangements, also known as interest-free finance, have become extremely popular recently. You will no doubt recognise the names of some of the players in this area as they advertise so heavily. According to ASIC, payments using these services more than doubled in 2020.

Buy-now-pay-later services allow you to buy a product now and pay it off in regular payments over a period of time, usually two or three months. It's a bit like old-school lay-by, only you get to take the product home (or have it delivered) immediately. They are not strictly loans, as most don't charge interest.

These companies make their money on some combination of fees charged to retailers, administration fees charged to customers, and late fees or penalty interest charged to customers who fail to meet the agreed repayments.

These late penalties can be quite high. ASIC has reported that about one in five people using these services are missing repayments or struggling to make them. So before you decide to use one of these services, please ensure you will be able to pay the money back on time.

A strategy for managing personal loans

Once you know what type of loan you have and the options to pay the money back, you can use the compounding effect to pay the loan off quicker. I discuss how compounding works on investments in Chapter 3.

With loans, it works like this. After taking out a loan, your first few repayments will go most toward interest, with a small proportion of those payments reducing the *principal*, or capital, of the loan. However, any time you can make an extra, larger-than-standard repayment, that extra money will come straight off the capital. This reduces both the loan and the total amount of interest you will end up paying.

Here are some suggestions to help:

- **Increase each repayment amount by whatever you can afford.** This is especially beneficial if you have a variable rate loan on which there should be no penalty for paying it off sooner. Increasing each repayment by as little as 10 or 20 per cent could reduce your total interest cost substantially.

- **Increase the number of repayments.** In a similar fashion, if you can afford to make an extra one-off repayment early in the loan, you will reduce the time to pay off the loan (and therefore the interest cost) by 5 to 10 per cent.

- **Change from monthly to fortnightly repayments.** Making this simple adjustment effectively creates an additional month in the year. You'll be making 26 fortnightly repayments (equivalent to 13 months) instead of 12 monthly repayments. That extra 'month' is effectively an extra repayment.

- **Consolidate multiple loans or credit card debts into a single personal loan.** This is worth considering as a way of getting control of these debts. If some of your personal loan debts are high interest or have high late-payment penalties, this consolidation will probably reduce your overall payment for these loans.

Home mortgages

As a member of the sandwich generation, I'm going to guess that taking out your first home mortgage is not at the top of your mind. Rather, you might be well down the path of paying that mortgage off, or perhaps you've already paid it off.

However, particularly if you have an outstanding mortgage, there are a few factors that need to be considered the closer you get to a possible retirement.

Note: I focus the discussion here on home mortgages. In Chapter 4 on building wealth through investments, I discuss taking out new mortgages on investment properties.

Retiring with debt...something to be avoided!

The advent of 30-year mortgages, which largely replaced 25-year mortgages in order to make the payments lower and more affordable, has led to a concerning trend for the sandwich generation. More and more people are finding themselves retiring with debt.

As I mentioned earlier, a home mortgage isn't, in itself, a 'bad debt', given it puts a roof over your head and supports an asset that, hopefully, is gaining value over time.

However, as a general rule, if you are in your 40s or 50s and still maintain a mortgage on your home, the aim should be to have this paid off before you retire. If at all possible, you want to avoid counting on your superannuation savings to pay down that debt. To do so would be to enter your retirement from well behind the starting line.

To work out what adjustments you need to make to your current repayments in order to pay off your loan, use a mortgage calculator (see the ASIC Moneysmart website, for example). If increasing your repayments by, say, 30 per cent is too much at the moment, start with an extra 10 or 20 per cent.

Pay whatever you can afford. At least if you do the calculation, you know what you're up against and have something to aim for.

Here are two other helpful hints for reducing your mortgage:

- **If there is an interest rate cut and your lender reduces your required repayments, maintain your repayments at the previous level.** It may be a small difference, but it is extra principal coming off your loan each time.

- **Consider shifting to fortnightly rather than monthly repayments, especially if that is the way your salary is paid.** Paying half the monthly rate every two weeks effectively adds an additional monthly payment into each year (as there are 26 fortnights in a year).

Consider the difference that paying extra off your mortgage makes in this example:

REDUCING YOUR MORTGAGE EXAMPLE

	Standard	Paying an extra $2000 per month
Mortgage	$1 000 000	$1 000 000
Repayments (monthly)	$4,300	$6,300
Interest rate (per annum)	3%	3%
Mortgage term	30 years	17 years
Principal and interest	$1 535 000	$1 300 000
Savings in interest		**$235 000**
Savings in time		**13 years**

At the end of the day, it's important to remember the basis for any good long-term financial plan is to retire comfortably. That should mean retiring with either no debt or debt only against investment assets such as shares or property—debts that are worth more than the loan and that provide an income through distributions or rent. Ideally that income will pay off all, or the majority, of the loan for you.

Making sure you're getting the best deal

Regardless of the status of your current mortgage, here's an important tip: take the time to review your mortgage every three or four years. Contact your bank or mortgage broker and ask whether your current arrangement is the best they can do for you. If not, be willing to refinance with another lender. You would be surprised how few people do this, and how often a bank will review a loan in your favour if you have been banking with them for a while.

Reverse mortgages: A special case

A reverse mortgage is similar to a home loan, but whereas in a traditional mortgage the funds are used to buy the house that is mortgaged (that is, your own home), with a reverse mortgage those funds can be used for other purposes.

For instance, you might take out a reverse mortgage to release a lump sum (say 5 to 20 per cent of the value of your home) that can help you maintain your post-retirement standard of living without having to sell your home. With a typical reverse mortgage, there is no need to make regular payments.

Interest simply accrues on the loan, and the original sum plus interest is repaid when you eventually sell your house (or pass away).

This all sounds great in theory, as you are unlocking the value you've built up in your home without having to sell the home. It sounds even more attractive if your home is your only substantial asset but your superannuation is insufficient to provide you with the income you need to live on.

When reverse mortgages first became popular in the 1990s, there were few consumer protections or limits in place. Unfortunately, in some extreme cases, retirees found themselves owing the whole value of their house, or even more as the debt kept increasing over time.

Today there are limits in place as to what proportion of your home's value you can borrow and there are caps on how much needs to ever be repaid. These limits provide much greater protection to the consumer.

However, as a general rule reverse mortgages should only be considered as a last resort. The last thing you want in your retirement is a growing debt. Should you consider going down this path, I strongly suggest you seek financial advice before making any decisions.

Wrangling bad debt

Getting control of a bad debt situation is quite simple in theory, but it can be quite difficult in practice.

Before we move on, the first point I would make is that if you are struggling with a serious debt challenge it is important to seek advice. A good place to start is the National Debt Helpline (ndh.org.au, 1800 007 007), a government supported, not-for-profit service providing free professional financial counselling. Be wary of 'advice' services attached to organisations that sell loan consolidation products. Everyone's debt situation is different, so getting personalised advice can be worthwhile, especially if your situation is complex.

The first step to taking back control of your debt is to understand where your money is going, as we discussed in Chapter 1. You must understand where and what you are spending money on and where you can cut back.

Changing your spending habits will be an important step in turning your situation around and avoiding going into further debt.

The second step is to look at your total debt and consider consolidation where appropriate. This is where seeking advice can be useful, because the numbers may not be as simple as they seem.

For instance, if you have a credit card debt of $20 000 at 20 per cent interest per annum plus a $400 000 mortgage (at 4 per cent per annum interest) on an $800 000 home, it would seem sensible to draw down on the mortgage to pay off the credit card debt. That would reduce the effective interest rate on that $20 000 to only 4 per cent per annum. However, by moving the debt into your mortgage, the risk is that you will pay it off slowly, potentially over 25 years. This may cost you more in the long term.

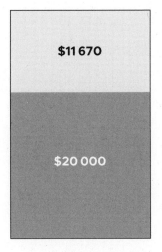
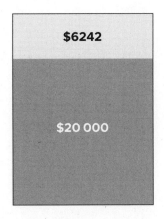

Paying $20 000 at
4% per annum over 25 years

Paying $20 000 at
20% per annum over 3 years

The interest cost on $20 000 at 4 per cent per annum over 25 years would be $11 670. Compare that with the interest cost of $20 000 at 20 per cent per annum over three years at $6242. In this scenario, remaining focused on the credit card debt and paying it off as soon as possible may be the better option.

My point here is that it is not only the interest rate that is important, but also the length of time over which the debt will be paid off.

Of course, the critical point either way is to avoid building up even more debt—which means revisiting the 'basics' in Chapter 1.

Your action plan and next steps

☐ List all your debts, including what interest rates you are paying.

☐ Start a plan to pay them off as soon as practical to save on interest.

☐ Going forward, only borrow on credit for what you can pay back in full in around 10 months, not on what the upper limit of the credit card is.

In Chapter 10, I share a full 12-month action plan incorporating many of these actions. In addition, my website (themoneysandwich.com) has plenty of templates, calculators and general information to help you with this process.

Josh and Liz's story — the best house in the street

Josh and Liz always took pride in their home. They genuinely felt they had the best in the street, and they wanted it to stay that way. It wasn't quite a case of 'keeping up with the Joneses', but they definitely kept an eye on what their neighbours were up to with any renovations.

Josh and Liz both worked hard and earned good salaries. When they both turned 50, they found they had a choice to make after their two adult children moved out of the family home. The couple found themselves with extra income available now that they had stopped paying school and university fees and their day-to-day living costs only needed to cover the two of them.

They still owed $150 000 on the mortgage on their single-storey home. The house had a new kitchen and bathroom, both of which Josh and Liz had financed out of their savings, though this had left their savings account fairly bare. They both had modest superannuation savings — not enough to retire on yet, but they planned to work for the next 15 years as they still enjoyed their jobs.

After one of their neighbours added a second storey to their home, Josh and Liz did some research and decided doing the same might be a good idea.

Josh was especially keen to do this. He'd read that their own home was capital gains tax free, so there would be no tax to pay on the proceeds of the sale when they sold it. Why not borrow more and add value to their home?

The cost of the extension was going to be $600000. By taking out a new mortgage and choosing a 30-year term over the 25-year term, the monthly repayments would be manageable and they'd still have enough coming in to enjoy a good social life.

As it happened, Liz's father, Nino, had always been interested in property.

He had a portfolio of investment properties that provided him with enough income to live off in his retirement. Just before they went ahead, the couple decided to seek out Nino's advice. He created two scenarios for them to compare.

Scenario 1: Add the second storey (for $600000) as planned

The *advantage* of this option was that it would add value to Josh and Liz's home, and enable them to retain their crown for having the best property in the street.

However, there were a few *disadvantages* as well. First, the project would add another $600000 to their existing mortgage, which they would be paying off until they were 80 — 15 years after they retired. An alternative would be to pay off the loan from their superannuation after they retired, but that would have drastically reduced their post-retirement income and living standards. Or it would force them to sell the home they loved in the street they loved in order to downsize into a different area. That would have felt like starting again. What's more, they didn't need the extra room of the upper storey, not to mention having to live through the inconvenience of such a major renovation.

Scenario 2: Take out a similar loan but spend the money on an investment property

The main *advantage* of this approach was that it would add another asset to their retirement portfolio (in addition to their super)—an asset that would likely grow in value and provide ongoing income. With rental payments contributing to their loan repayments, they would be able to pay the loan off more quickly—likely before they retired. What's more, with continuing rental income after they retired, in addition to their super, they would improve their retirement standard rather than decrease it—without the need to sell their current home. All they had to do was come to terms with the idea that their house may not be the best in the street any longer.

The *disadvantage* of this option was that it would increase Josh and Liz's debt level. However, that debt would be offset by the value of the investment property, the value of which would grow over time if they bought wisely. They wouldn't have a second storey and so their house wouldn't be worth as much as if they chose Option 1. However, with just the two of them, they didn't need that, and leaving their home as it was would involve less upkeep and they wouldn't have to live through the renovation.

Josh and Liz's decision

After Nino explained all this to Josh and Liz, their enthusiasm for the idea of adding a second storey diminished. Nino pointed out that going down that path would have made Josh and Liz 'asset rich but cash poor'.

Josh then recalled friends who had kept investing in their homes right through to retirement, only to find themselves with few savings, not much in their superannuation and forced to downsize before they chose to do so on their own terms.

PART 2

Planning for financial freedom

The next three chapters focus on what should be a central aim for any member of the sandwich generation: maximising your financial freedom up to and beyond 'Year R'.

What's 'Year R'? It's what is traditionally called your retirement age — what most people think of when they think of their 65th birthday.

Why not just call it the retirement age? Because it's not that simple, or at least it doesn't need to be. While some people certainly get to the age of 65 (or thereabouts) with the full intention of leaving paid work for good, an increasing number of people like to keep their options open. Some love their job so much that they choose to continue in paid work for as long as they can. Others stay in paid work but scale things back — to a few days a week, for instance.

Of those who choose to finish up their career, some look to go into volunteer work, some want to start something entirely different (turning a hobby into a business, for example), and some want to travel as much as they can. Some decide to live the life of the retirement brochures, playing golf during the day and walking along the beach hand-in-hand with their partner every evening.

What we're really talking about here is *lifestyle* and the *mental/emotional* factors behind the question of retirement. These are very important to think about *before* you think about your financial situation. Once you know what you would like to be doing with the post-'Year R' stage of your life, you'll be in a better position to do some planning. Financial freedom means knowing that whichever path you choose, the money isn't going to run out... but to work that out, you need to choose a path first.

In Chapter 3 ('Laying the groundwork'), I cover those areas you need to consider before you create a plan for financial freedom, including establishing where you are today and where you want to be, and thinking about your risk profile.

Following that, in Chapter 4 ('Building an investment portfolio'), I look at investment planning and strategies in general: what you can do to maximise your wealth in the years leading up to 'Year R' and beyond.

Finally, in Chapter 5 ('Optimising for retirement'), I delve into superannuation.

It's important that you read this part in its entirety, for two reasons. First, many of the investment options or strategies described apply to both super and non-super investing. Second, while superannuation is a topic most people associate with retirement, making the most of it requires some planning pre-retirement, or pre- 'Year R', ideally around 10 years out as a minimum.

3

Laying the groundwork

What's in this chapter

Setting your financial freedom target

Assessing your risk profile

How Father Time helps us all

To this point we have discussed taking control of your money and getting to grips with debt. You can consider these the prerequisites for what follows, which is all about planning for your future and that of your family. Having control of your spending and debt makes it easier to see what options you have in front of you.

Many people never reach this point. Like Andrew and Rebecca in the Introduction, they find it hard enough keeping up with the here and now, let alone finding time to make plans for their futures. This is completely understandable, but as an adviser I have to tell you that even a small amount of planning effort ahead of time can make all the difference to how comfortable you will be in retirement.

In this chapter, we focus on gaining an understanding of your current financial position and the gap between that and what you will need to provide you with a comfortable retirement, whatever that may look like.

In the following chapters we'll get into the details of making investments, building superannuation and creating retirement strategies.

The big points: Your investment plan

What you can do right now, no questions asked

1. Create a quick summary of your financial position in terms of assets and liabilities for yourself (and your partner if you're doing this together). At this stage it doesn't need to be highly accurate. A back-of-the-envelope effort will do, or use the template on our website (themoneysandwich.com). You can also find a simple online tool for this on the ASIC Moneysmart website (search for 'net worth calculator'). Your aim at this point is not to make any judgement about your position but simply to be aware of it—something most people aren't.

2. Draft a plan with set goals and dreams for your future. This doesn't need to be detailed either; preferably, it will fit on a single piece of paper. This can be done on your own or with the help of a trusted adviser. I have tips on how to do this further on. Once you've created your draft plan, display it somewhere where you will be able to see it, such as on your fridge. Don't hold back on doing this because you think you'll be making commitments you may not be able to keep. The idea of this document is that it will continue to live and evolve. The reality is that no matter what the plan, having it documented will increase your chances of achieving it.

3. Work out your 'financial freedom' number. This is the amount of income you'll need each year, post-Year R and for the rest of your life, in order to live comfortably. Is it $60 000 per year, or $100 000 per year? A rule of thumb is to take two-thirds of the amount you are living on now, while still working, as a good starting point for discussion.

4. Complete the Risk Profile Self-Assessment questionnaire (see the later section 'Risk profile self-assessment'). Your risk profile will be an important factor in your investment plan, as it guides the types of investment you might consider and/or what proportion of your money you will be willing to invest and in what types of investment.

Setting your financial freedom target

Before you get into any detail in your plan for financial freedom, you need to spend a little time establishing where you are now, financially speaking; where you'll be at Year R if nothing changes; where you want to be by Year R; and how to close any gap between the two. There are four steps to this.

1. Capture your current and projected financial positions

Your current position

After the work of getting control of your money and debt, gaining a clear understanding your *current* financial position represents another step towards being on top of your money. This is particularly important for those of us in the sandwich generation, for whom things have normally grown at least a little complicated; by now, you've been in the workforce for 30 to 40 years and you may have collected a range of assets and liabilities.

The Your Financial Position form (which you can download from themoneysandwich.com) provides an easy way to record your financial position as it is now, and to keep track of it into the future on a monthly basis. The idea is to update the form monthly, and start a clean form at the beginning of each year.

YOUR FINANCIAL POSITION

	July 2020	August 2020	Ongoing ...
ASSETS			
Bank account 1	$10 000	$10 200	
Bank account 2	$2000	$1500	
Super fund 1	$400 000	$407 000	
Super fund 2	$100 000	$103 000	
Shares	$28 000	$29 000	
Bonds	–	–	
Home	$1 200 000	$1 200 000	
Investment property	–	–	
Other (car etc.)	–	–	
Total assets	**$1 740 000**	**$1 750 700**	
LIABILITIES			
Credit card 1	$2000	$1700	
Credit card 2	$1000	$900	
Loan — car	$10 000	$9500	
Loan — personal	–	–	
Mortgage 1	$250 000	$247 000	
Mortgage 2	–	–	
Other	–	–	
Total debts	**$263 000**	**$259 100**	
Net position	**$1 477 000**	**$1 491 600**	

Your projected retirement position

Assuming you're not ready to retire just yet, your current financial position won't give you a complete picture of what things will look like when you reach retirement age. Hopefully between now and then you'll be able to build your savings to improve your position. At the very least, assuming you are in steady work, you would expect to build your superannuation balance through the growth of that investment plus your employer's contributions over the coming years.

For the 'investment growth' part of this equation, you use the 'rule of 72' to estimate how much you can expect your existing super balance to increase before you reach retirement age. Dividing the number 72 by the average rate of return you expect to earn will give you a rough idea of how long it will take to double that balance. For instance, for a rate of return of 7 per cent pa, your money will double in about $72 \div 7 = 10.2$ years. (The 'rule of 72' provides rough guidance only. It doesn't take into account other factors such as inflation, market conditions, and so on.)

Considering the number of years until you reach retirement age, you can use this rule to estimate what your current superannuation savings will be worth by that time.

Adding that number to the savings you expect to be able to accrue over that period, plus the superannuation contributions that will be made, will give you what we can call your *current projected retirement position*. (There's a worked example in the forthcoming step 3 that might make this clearer.)

2. Capture your goals

Making the most of the wealth you already have requires an overall plan and an investment strategy.

But you can't create these until you have worked out what your goals are. Your plan and investment strategy can then be built to support your goals.

Life and financial goals are a very personal thing, but broadly they might include things like 'retire comfortably', 'travel more' and/or 'pay for the grandchildren's education'.

Whatever your goals are, they need to be written down, along with when you would like to achieve them by and, for goals with a financial component, how much they will cost.

Let's look at an example of a single goal:

1. **Goal:** To retire on $60000 per annum (your 'financial freedom' number).

2. **Timing:** I want to be able to do this in 10 years from now.

3. **Cost:** Using a rule of thumb that you'll need around 20 times your desired retirement income, the money needed to achieve this goal is $1200000.

Repeat this calculation for three or four goals in total. For major financial goals, keeping it to three seems to work best.

Here's an example set of goals for a couple in their mid-50s:

Your goals	When by	How much	Total
1. Retire comfortably	1 January, 2030	$60000 per annum	$1200000
2. School fees for grandchildren	1 February, 2035	$100000 total	$100000
3. Holiday travel every year	1 January, 2030	$15000 per annum	$300000
Tip: as a rule of thumb, multiply annual amount by 20 before adding to total. (Assume 5% per annum income over long-term.)			**$1600000**

Obviously setting specific dates, down to the day, is guesswork to some extent when you're looking 10 to 20 years ahead. Nevertheless, I think it is worth doing to make those dates feel more concrete. Visit themoneysandwich.com for a Capture Your Goals template.

3. Identify your retirement gap

Once you know your current position and your *current projected retirement position* (your current position plus future savings) and you've quantified your goals, the next step is to work out the gap between the two. That information can then be used to develop an investment strategy to either maintain your current position or make up the difference between where you will be if nothing changes, and where you want to be.

When most people do this exercise, they find themselves falling short; that is, they have a *retirement gap*. If they just leave things as they are, they'll reach Year R without the resources they need to achieve their retirement goals.

This is where planning and strategy come in: working out how you can reduce that gap to reach your targets.

Let's take an example:

Where are you now	
Home*	$1 200 000
Super fund 1	$400 000
Super fund 2	$100 000
Cash/shares	$40 000
Total	**$540 000**

• *Home not included in total for this example, unless planning to downsize in the future*

Time frame	10 years

(continued)

'Rule of 72' calculation (assumes 7% per annum return for this example)	
$540 000 doubles in 10 years	$1 080 000

Future employer contributions	
Super contributions in 10 years	$200 000
Total	**$1 280 000**

Your retirement goals	**$1 600 000**

RETIREMENT GAP	$320 000

To help work out your own retirement scenario, you can use the Your Retirement Gap calculator on our website (themoneysandwich.com).

It's important to understand that this is just a rule of thumb and not to be considered accurate, as it is very much educated guesswork. It does not take into consideration factors such as inflation, fluctuating returns, life events, and so on. It is only intended to provide some guidance on setting goals and what to consider in your future planning.

4. Build a plan to close the gap

Creating a plan to close your retirement gap will likely mean making some adjustments to your current approach to saving, and to any investment strategies you currently have.

It might involve finding more to save, increasing your super contributions, changing your investment strategy to get a better return, borrowing to invest, or a combination of these and more. (We'll be looking at all these options in chapters 4 and 5.)

The more time you have on your side, the more options you have available to you, so the sooner you act the better.

A successful plan will build on the newfound control of your finances you discovered in Part 1 of this book, giving you control of not only the 'now' but into the future.

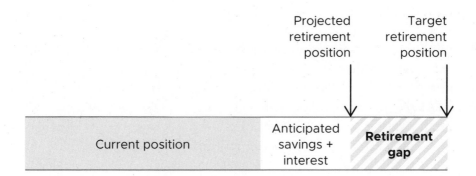

Assessing your risk profile

Before you start actively making financial plans, particularly with respect to investments, it's important to assess your understanding of and tolerance for risk. If you work with a financial adviser, they will do this as a matter of course: they are required to do so before making any investment recommendations to their clients.

What do we mean by risk in the context of financial planning?

Every time you make an investment, it comes with a level of risk that the underlying entity you are investing in may not perform to your expectations. Share prices rise and fall, often for reasons that have little to do with the value of the underlying company. Some share prices rise and fall more than others due to volatility in the underlying company's industry (for example, bank shares tend to be more stable than resource shares because the latter are more affected by global commodity prices).

There is an oft-repeated rule of thumb when it comes to investments: *the higher the return, the higher the risk*. In other words, to achieve potentially higher returns, you have to be prepared to accept a higher risk of volatility and/or capital loss. The opposite is also true: you can make very low-risk investments by, say, putting your money in the bank, but you are likely to earn relatively low returns on those investments.

All of this comes down to what we call the 'risk/return trade off', and only you can decide what level of risk you are prepared to accept in return for the possibility of higher returns. We call this your 'risk tolerance' or 'risk profile'. Someone with a low or conservative risk profile will be more comfortable in lower risk investments, whereas someone with a more aggressive risk profile will be happier to put their money into more volatile investments with the potential for higher returns.

Regardless of where you sit on this line, understanding your risk profile will be an important factor in choosing investments as part of your investment strategy.

Don't equate a high-risk investment strategy with 'sure thing' opportunities

When I talk about higher risk in terms of an investment strategy, I'm talking about building a diverse portfolio of investments likely to pay off over the longer term. This is very different to the high risk associated with putting all your money, or a large part of it, into a single speculative investment, such as a start-up company or some other 'sure thing' that you heard about from a mate at the pub. That sort of investment is not strategic — it's gambling.

Rather than risking a dip in value, you are likely risking the complete loss of your investment. If you do want to take advantage of such an 'opportunity', firstly make sure you understand the actual risks (never believe anyone who says there is no risk) and are comfortable with them. Secondly, limit the amount you invest to, as a general rule, no more than 10 per cent of your portfolio.

Risk profile self-assessment

The Risk Profile Self-Assessment questionnaire is a simple exercise that can give you a starting point for understanding your own risk profile and tolerance when it comes to investing. My view is that with education and a better understanding of investments, your risk profile should progress towards high growth rather than defensive, especially if you have time on your side.

A starter's guide to working out what type of investor you are

To achieve potentially higher returns over time, you will have to be prepared to accept a higher risk of volatility. This is because investments that offer higher returns — such as shares — are generally more volatile, especially in the short term, than those producing lower returns, such as cash or bonds.

1. How long do you expect to be able to invest before you need access to your money?

    A. Less than one year

    B. One to three years

    C. Three to seven years

    D. Greater than seven years

2. Have you invested in shares and/or property before?

    A. No

    B. Yes, but I have only a limited understanding

    C. Yes, I understand the concept of holding a share/property portfolio

    D. Yes, I have full knowledge of holding a share/property portfolio

3. How concerned are you about inflation eroding your investment portfolio's growth?

   A. Not concerned as I will only invest in cash

   B. Somewhat concerned

   C. Concerned

   D. Very concerned

4. While sharemarkets have always trended upwards over the long term, they do drop from time to time. What level of reduction of the value of your investment portfolio or superannuation savings are you prepared to accept in a year?

   A. None

   B. Up to 10 per cent

   C. Between 10 and 20 per cent

   D. More than 20 per cent

5. Investment risk summary: Which of the following do you feel best describes you?

   A. Security of capital is essential to me as I never want to see a negative return

   B. A small degree of risk would be acceptable for a slight increase in potential returns

   C. A moderate degree of risk would be acceptable in return for the potential for increased returns

   D. A high degree of risk is acceptable to me as I always invest for the long term and understand how markets work and that they can be volatile.

Based on your answers to these questions, you can grade your approximate attitude to risk on the following scale:

Only (A)	Conservative	For investors who mainly want preservation of fixed assets (cash, fixed incomes, bonds etc.).
Mainly (A) and (B)	Moderately conservative	For investors who want a more diverse mix of assets, however still being cautious.
Mainly (B) and (C)	Balanced	For investors who want a balanced level of security and growth.
Mainly (D)	Growth	For investors who are willing to invest more in growth assets and have the possibility of a higher investment return for greater risk or volatility.
Only (D)	High-growth	For investors who are more knowledgeable in their investing, relying on high-growth assets to potentially provide larger returns in the long term.

In Chapter 4, where I discuss various investment options, I also look at the risk levels associated with those options, using terminology similar to this scale—from conservative to high growth.

How Father Time helps us all

We've all been tempted at one time or another by the chance of a quick win: the bet on the Melbourne Cup outsider you got the 'word' on from a mate; the chip placed on your lucky number at the roulette table; or the ticket in a $15 million PowerBall lottery. There's nothing wrong with any of these as an occasional flutter—provided you understand that they are all forms of gambling, not investment.

'Quick wins' and investment are essentially mutually exclusive. Quick wins happen once in a while, but those occasions are best regarded as flukes.

When it comes to realising the potential of an investment, *time* is an essential part of the equation. We need to put aside any illusions of winning quickly and instead choose good-quality investments, then let time do its thing. Time—the longer the better—smooths out the ups and downs of recessions, natural disasters, changes of government (and government policy) and all the other factors that can cause market volatility. In short, giving an investment time smooths out short-term complications.

This also applies to you, the investor. Daily (or hourly!) checking of the value of your share investments is the easiest way to needlessly increase your stress levels. When you take a long-term mindset, you can shrug off even significant falls in the market, safe in the knowledge that by the time you want to sell, it more than likely will have bounced back past where it started. (By the end of 2020, the Australian sharemarket had recovered almost all the losses it incurred at the outbreak of the COVID-19 pandemic and during the oil crisis in March 2020. The US market had exceeded that point, despite the fact that the pandemic still had a long way to run.)

There are only two prices that matter with any investment you make: the price you buy it for, and the price you sell it at. Everything in between is noise.

The effect of inflation on our investments

Inflation is the general increase in the price of goods and services over time, which reflects a reduction in the purchasing power of your dollars. Where a trip to the cinema in the 1960s might have cost around 10 cents, that same 10 cents today might only buy you a couple of raspberry lollies in the cinema's foyer. That's inflation.

In Australia, household inflation is measured by the Consumer Price Index (CPI), which is reported quarterly.

Inflation affects investments because it reduces the effective returns they provide. At a minimum, your investments need to provide a return large enough to offset that loss of purchasing power. If inflation is running at, say, 3 per cent per annum, you'll need a 3 per cent interest rate on your bank account just to 'break even'.

This is one reason why it's a myth that keeping your money under the bed is the safest place for it. Keep it under there long enough and within a few years its real value will be considerably reduced.

When looking at real or potential returns on your investments, always consider the reported returns against the inflation rate at the time. Your *net* return is the investment return less the inflation rate. For instance, in the compounding interest example in the next section, I assume a 7 per cent per annum return and an inflation rate of 3 per cent, equating to a 4 per cent net return.

At the time of writing, inflation is at historically very low levels—less than 1 per cent—which is why it is rarely a topic of discussion. In the longer term, it is unlikely to stay this low and will more than likely be worthy of consideration again. You should bear it in mind when trying to gain a true picture of how well your investments—of any sort—are performing.

The power of compounding interest

The most powerful example of the impact of time is 'compounding'. You've probably heard the term—you probably did an example in your maths class in around Year 8. However, there's a good chance that since then you've forgotten its significance. *Compounding interest* is the principle of reinvesting the returns generated by your investments, which allows those returns to start generating their own earnings. This is where your money really starts working for you. Understanding and using the principles of compounding is the secret to really substantial investment growth.

It works like this. Imagine you make an investment of $1000 which grows 10 per cent in one year. That growth means you will have earned an extra $100 simply by having your money working for you. Now, if you leave that balance of $1100 ($1000 + $100 interest) untouched for the following year (rather than withdrawing and spending the $100), you'll earn interest in that year on both the original $1000 and on the extra $100. So in the second year (assuming the same rate of return) you'll earn $110 in interest. Now you have $1210 in your account, which in the next year again will earn $121 in interest. And so on. Every year, the amount of interest earned will be higher than in the year before.

The impact of compounding can be substantial. Leave that investment in place (again assuming a constant rate of return) for 25 years and the interest earned in a single year will be as much as the original investment.

Let's look at a practical example. Imagine you are wanting to set aside some savings for your grandchildren's private secondary school fees. The following table shows two potential approaches: contributing $7000 to a fund each year for 10 years, or $5000 each year for 17 years, in both cases reinvesting all earnings (which for this example is set at 7 per cent per annum).

In the first approach (Savings 1), by the time the child starts school there is already enough money in the account to fund six years of schooling. The interest the account earns adds enough each year to prevent the savings being eaten away too quickly. In the end, you've paid out $70000 to fund $136090 worth of fees. The magic of compounding has saved you $66090. The savings of the other approach (Savings 2) are not quite as high, but they are still substantial.

Age	Future school fees	Savings 1	Account balance	Savings 2	Account balance
1		$7000	$7490	$5000	$5350
2		$7000	$15 504	$5000	$11 075
3		$7000	$24 080	$5000	$17 200
4		$7000	$33 255	$5000	$23 754
5		$7000	$43 073	$5000	$30 766
6		$7000	$53 578	$5000	$38 270
7		$7000	$64 819	$5000	$46 299
8		$7000	$76 846	$5000	$54 890
9		$7000	$89 715	$5000	$64 082
10		$7000	$103 485	$5000	$73 918
11		$7000	$110 729	$5000	$84 442
12	$20 986		$97 494	$5000	$74 717
13	$21 637		$82 682	$5000	$63 660
14	$22 308		$66 162	$5000	$51 159
15	$22 999		$47 794	$5000	$37 091
16	$23 712		$27 427	$5000	$21 325
17	$24 447		$4900	$5000	$3720
Total	$136 090	$70 000		$85 000	
	You save	$66 090		$51 089	

Assumed:
Fees (today) — $15 000
Inflation — 3% per annum
Interest — 7% per annum

Here is a visual of the spreadsheet for the Savings 2 approach to give you a better idea of how compounding interest works.

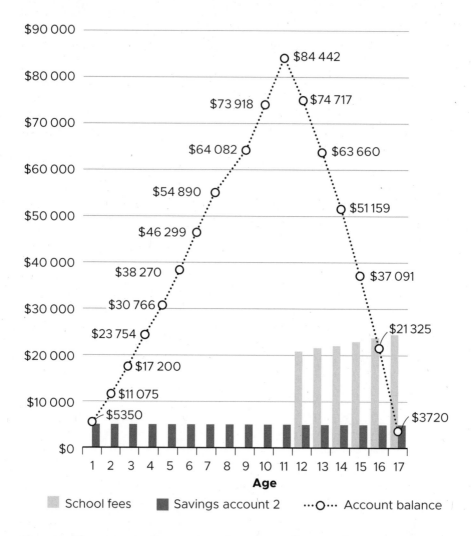

You could use a similar approach to save for any longer-term goal, whether that be travel, a major purchase or anything else.

This principle applies to any form of investment in which your returns are reinvested as they are earned. This can include savings accounts, term deposits (rolled over at the end of each term), managed funds, investment platforms and even individual shares with a dividend reinvestment option.

The bottom line: whatever investments you make, do everything you can to reinvest your earnings. Put your money to work and let 'compounding and time' take care of the rest.

Your action plan and next steps

☐ Complete the Your Financial Position template (see themoneysandwich .com), and start a habit of updating this monthly or quarterly.

☐ Write down your future goals, how much they will cost and the time frame.

☐ Work out your retirement gap. (The next chapters will help you work out how to best close that gap.)

☐ Complete the Risk Profile Self-Assessment questionnaire as it is important to understand your risk profile before you change any of your investments around.

In Chapter 10, I share a full 12-month action plan incorporating many of these actions. In addition, my website (themoneysandwich.com) has plenty of templates, calculators and general information to help you with this process.

Jamila's story — we all need a plan

Jamila's story is one that, unfortunately, is not atypical of the people we see at a very difficult time in their lives. In Jamila's case a major shift to her life came not through the death or illness of her partner, but as a result of a divorce in her mid-50s. However, the lessons Jamila learnt were relevant to any of these situations.

On top of all the personal and lifestyle challenges Jamila faced, she had a number of financial hurdles to get past, including:

- Dealing with financial and related matters when she had never done that in the past. (Like most couples, one of the pair tended to look after this stuff, and in Jamila's case it was her husband.)

- Trying to manage the assets she had received in the divorce settlement, which included some cash (as a lump sum) and various investments. Like Jamila, many people are terrified that they'll mismanage the money and see it disappear too quickly as they never get over the fear of taking that first step to actively manage it.

- Wanting to maintain the lifestyle of herself and her teenage children, including ensuring that the kids could finish their schooling with as little disruption as possible.

- Wanting to support her children after school as much as possible.

Typical of people like herself, while Jamila had received an equitable settlement from the divorce, she did not see this as a windfall. Rather, it caused her stress because she did not feel prepared to deal with it. Various advice from well-meaning friends and relatives only made the situation worse by adding to Jamila's existing confusion.

Finally, Jamila sought professional help by coming to see us. Here are some of the things we worked through with her.

Establishing the basics

At our first meeting we really didn't spend a lot of time talking about money at all. We needed to know about Jamila and her family and their current situation, at a broad level. We encouraged her to think about her objectives in the short and medium term — her broad life goals rather than just her financial objectives. Did she want to return to work, for instance? This conversation not only helped us establish the 'lay of the land', but it was also useful for Jamila to stand back and consider her situation holistically — not just from a legal or financial point of view.

Providing reassurance

Another component of the first meeting in these situations is to provide support at a very stressful time.

Most financial situations can be navigated with appropriate planning, and there are always options. Without going into too much detail (and importantly, without using financial jargon) at this point, we do like to provide reassurance that we should be able to help them through this.

In addition, people like Jamila need to understand that just because they find all this financial stuff overwhelming, that doesn't make them stupid or ignorant in any way. Clearly a smart person, Jamila felt she should have been more on top of her financial situation. This was an unrealistic expectation to put on herself — there is enough to stay on top of in work and life without being up to date on the stuff that someone else (Jamila's former husband, in her case) is managing perfectly well. So, with that in mind, we encouraged Jamila to ask as many questions as she needed to, and to understand that there is no such thing as a stupid question.

Laying the ground rules for advice

One of the things we often have to manage for people in Jamila's situation is what I call the 'I know a guy' scenario. We've all seen it, if we haven't experienced it ourselves. It's the situation where a friend or family member—even someone you've just met—claims to have the inside running on a wonderful investment option. The opportunity is so good, they tell you, that they've put all their money into it (or at least they think you should).

When people come to us to discuss these 'opportunities' (and hopefully they do seek professional advice before taking them up), our answer is always very simple: don't do it.

A golden rule: never, ever, put all your eggs in one basket.

Diversity is always important, as no single investment will ever be perfect and no one should ever put their life savings in just one place.

Unfortunately, people in Jamila's situation can be overwhelmed with unsolicited advice, which only adds to the anxiety they are feeling already.

The only advice you really need in a situation like this is to seek professional advice. Ignore the once-in-a-lifetime opportunities, but do ask friends and family if they have a financial adviser themselves and who they're happy with. If not, Chapter 10 explains the ways to source a financial adviser and what to look for.

Making a plan

After the initial conversations with Jamila, aimed primarily at getting to know each other, providing reassurance and thinking about immediate next steps, we set up further meetings to start making a plan that would help her achieve her short-term and longer-term goals. Many of these had a financial focus, of course, given that is my specialty. However, I strongly believe that a good adviser will also maintain a view on their clients' hopes and dreams beyond the purely financial. As well as simply taking a holistic point of view, it has a practical purpose. Understanding someone's motivations is an important component of knowing what will and won't work for them in terms of their investment strategy.

If we've done our job properly in the initial stages, this planning stage can provide a concrete path forward, which in turn provides comfort and reassurance. The details of the plan will be different in every case, but suffice to say that many of the elements discussed in this book will form part of it.

Once Jamila has a plan, including a strategy to help her reach her goals, and we have ensured that she now understands what to do, the next step is to put in place an ongoing commitment to help her get there. Just as with most new year's resolutions, people left to their own devices tend to let their new intentions drift or disappear after a few months. That's why they need encouragement and coaching to help keep track of progress and 'maintain the line'. A plan is a great start, but we all need to be held accountable.

Building an investment portfolio

What's in this chapter

The ingredients of a good investment strategy

Shares as an investment

Property as an investment

Other investment options

Hopefully by the time you've reached this point of the book you have some clarity about the size of your 'retirement gap', some sense of your risk profile (and, if applicable, your partner's) and an understanding of the power of compounding.

In this chapter, we're going to dive into all the various investment options you have available to you, now and into the future.

Remember these two golden rules when choosing investments:

- **Past performance is no guarantee of future performance.** Just because an investment performed well last year there is no certainty it will do it again, so it is important to diversify.

- **Take advantage of 'compounding returns' and 'time' to turbocharge your investment savings.** It is the core aspect of any good plan to know where you are invested for what return, and give it time to succeed.

The big points: Your investment strategy

What you can do right now, no questions asked

1. In Chapter 3, you listed what assets you currently own, which possibly includes shares, managed funds, property and super. Do you know where these are invested and what level of risk or volatility is associated with them? Do you know how diverse your investments are, in terms of the type of investment, industry (for example, commodities, banks) and risk levels? Have you accrued these investments with any planning or just allowed them to run their own course? We'll cover all this in this chapter, but before we start it is worth reviewing your current situation.

2. If you have few or no assets other than your superannuation and possibly your home, but would like to expand, this is the time to do some research. Obviously, that starts with this book (and my website themoneysandwich.com)! And this chapter in particular. But if you have additional questions, the ASIC Moneysmart website is a good place to start. Your bank's website likely also has information on investing in shares and property, and so on. The more you know, the less the ups and downs of being an active investor will cause you anxiety or sleepless nights.

3. Check in with your partner about their understanding of investments such as shares and property. This knowledge often varies quite considerably within families, especially when one of you tends to 'look after the money stuff'. It is important that you are both up to speed so you can make any decisions together about super and investments for your future.

The ingredients of a good investment strategy

Here are eight important aspects of a good investment strategy for any plan. I will mention these repeatedly in this chapter and in Chapter 5:

1. **A good investment strategy will be consistent with your risk profile and tolerance.** There is little point in making higher-risk investments if it will lead you to have sleepless nights whenever there is a dip in the sharemarket. Hopefully the understanding of broader investing you gain from this book will give you greater comfort in making higher-risk/higher-return investments when appropriate.

2. **A good investment strategy will incorporate diversity.** Diversity in your investments means investing in a mixture of asset classes (for example, property, shares and cash), and further diversifying within those asset classes, such as investing in shareholdings across markets (Australian and international), in a range of industries or across a number of managed funds. Never invest all your money in one company!

3. **Always apply most of your investments to good-quality investments.** For shares, for example, this means blue chip companies: businesses that have stood the test of time and that will largely ride out the ups and downs of the market. For direct property investment, this means buying a well-built property in a good location that will be attractive to prospective tenants.

4. **Try to invest for the long term—usually seven to 10 years or more—where you can (that is, where it matches your goals).** The longer term your investments, the better placed they will be to ride out any market volatility. This is particularly the case with shares. As a rule of thumb, it is wise to expect a market drop about one year in every seven for property and around one year in every eight to 10 for shares. After the 2008 sharemarket fall at the onset of the Global Financial Crisis, it was 12 years until the 2020 market drop associated with oil and the COVID-19 pandemic. Historically, that is a long time between significant market falls.

5. **Look for a combination of income as well as capital growth.** When we are talking about investments for post-work financial independence, your ultimate aim is to have enough income generated by your investments and your superannuation to replace your salary.

6. **If your risk profile and tolerance allow it, don't be afraid of using good debt to your advantage.** Debt used wisely can help you build an investment asset base more quickly than if you rely solely on your own savings. This tactic is most commonly used for property investments due to the tax advantages of negative gearing (see the section 'Tax and property investments' later in this chapter); however, it can also be used with other asset classes such as shares or managed funds.

7. **Any good investment strategy has a tax component, so take advantage of tax minimisation opportunities where they are available.**

8. **You should invest to suit your own personal circumstances.** The information given in this book, or any other, can only ever be general. Everyone's risk profile or tolerance for risk is different, everyone's tax situation is different, and everyone's goals are different. You should seek the specific advice of a financial adviser or other appropriate professional before making any significant investment decisions.

Remember the difference between a good asset and a bad asset

The difference between a 'good' asset and a 'bad' asset, in terms of investments, is similar to the difference between good and bad debts.

A 'good' investment or asset is usually one that provides an income stream as well as growth over the medium to long term. While a car or boat may be a high-value asset, it is more likely a lifestyle choice (so 'bad' in investment terms), as its value starts to drop the moment you take it away from the dealer, and it doesn't provide any investment income like property or shares do.

Again, the caveat here is your own home. This can be categorised as a good investment simply because you need to live somewhere, and it's better in most cases to not be paying rent to someone else. Your own home also has tax advantages in not being liable for capital gains tax when you sell it.

Your investment options

Unless you're the sort of person who has actively invested in the past, your idea of 'investment' might be moving money from your transaction account to a savings account—or a term deposit, at a stretch. Beyond that, the idea of investing in shares or property may seem too complex to contemplate.

However, there are many options available these days that make investing much easier than it used to be. And given the very low interest rates on offer for most cash investments in recent times, it could be sensible to look further afield for better opportunities.

Before we start, and without wanting to get ahead of ourselves, you should be aware that most of the investment options described in the following sections are available both outside and inside superannuation. We'll come back to this, but hold that thought as you read on.

In the rest of this chapter, we'll look at the range of options available; however, we will concentrate on the two most utilised and popular areas of investment: shares and property.

Shares as an investment

Say the word 'investment' and many people will automatically think of shares. Shares are the rock stars of the investment world. They get most of the media attention. We all love a rags-to-riches story of speculation on a new stock whose value goes through the roof overnight. A fall in the market is front-page news.

Strip away all the hype and we can get back to the fundamental point that to own shares in a business is to own a part of that business. When the business makes a profit, as good businesses do, you, as a part owner, will share in that profit.

The reality is that sound share investments, considered over the medium to long term—say seven to 10 years plus—have consistently outperformed most other forms of investment, and especially cash, in terms of both income and capital growth. Add to this the fact that shares are easy to buy and sell, and don't require a very large investment to get started, and you can see why investing in shares is attractive to people at every stage of life.

Like property investments, share investments come with tax advantages, including negative gearing, where you borrow to invest (you can deduct any shortfall between the interest on the loan and income from share dividends), capital gains tax discounts and, unique to shares, so-called franking credits (see the section 'Tax and shares' later in this chapter).

Investing for income versus growth

It's important to understand the difference between income and capital growth when it comes to all investments, including shares. Depending on your investment strategy, you may choose to make investments that will favour one of these over the other in the shorter or longer term.

Capital growth

Variation in capital value—which can be either growth or loss—is the change in 'price' of an asset over time. For property, this is the change in the market value of the property. For shares, it's the change in the share price over time. The media tends to have an obsession with the capital value of shares, as reflected in the tracking of daily market movements and breathless reporting of 'crashes' as major disasters. Similarly, movements in house prices and auction clearance rates get a disproportionate amount of attention.

While capital growth is obviously desirable, it's important to remember that the value of an asset is only important on the day you buy it and the day you sell it. Everything in between is noise.

Income

In contrast to capital growth, the income that an asset produces is of ongoing importance for as long as you own that asset. For an investment property, income comes from rental payments. For shares, income equates to any *dividend*—effectively, a share of the profits—you are paid. When you own shares in reliable, profitable businesses—'blue chip' companies like BHP, the major banks and Telstra are good examples—then as a shareholder you will likely be paid a regular dividend (usually every six months). This income is effectively your share of the company's profit. While dividends will rise and fall with, say, the price that BHP can sell iron ore, in practice this variation is much less volatile than that of the share price.

As you approach Year R, it is likely that income will become more important than capital growth in your investments. Assuming that you won't be selling those investments to free up cash, your aim will be for the income from your investments (both inside and outside super) to replace as much of your salary as possible as you reduce the amount of paid work you do.

Options for owning shares

The traditional way to buy and sell shares was always to call a broker and have them make purchases and sales on the stock exchange on your behalf. That option is still available, though you are more likely to deal with your broker online than over the phone. However, today there are numerous other ways to access the sharemarket, some of which can provide greater diversity and liquidity with minimal effort on your part.

Direct shares

Direct investment in the publicly listed companies of your choice is quite straightforward. Opening an account with an online broker (often called an 'online trading account') is much the same as opening a bank account—even easier if you use your existing bank's trading service. Once your account opens, you will be able to place your own buy and sell orders. There will be a brokerage fee (around $20–$30) attached to each transaction.

For most people, direct share ownership will be a medium- to long-term component of their investment strategy.

Share trading, where people actively buy and sell shares on a daily basis in an attempt to anticipate and profit from small movements in the market, is a different game altogether. It is better seen as a form of gambling than a form of investment.

Advantages of direct share investing:

- You have complete flexibility to build your own portfolio exactly as you wish.

- There are no ongoing fees associated with share ownership.

- In some cases, you'll have the opportunity to reinvest dividends back into additional shares.

Disadvantages of direct share investing:

- Direct share investment can involve a significant amount of administration. You will receive regular statements (usually six monthly) from the share registry of each of the shares you own, and it will be your responsibility (or your accountant's) to report income and process the tax deductible franking credits (see the upcoming section 'Tax and shares') for each parcel of shares you own, along with tracking your capital gains/losses at the time you sell the shares.

- Investing in direct shares provides less diversity than some of the other investment options (such as property, gold, cryptocurrencies, term deposits and bonds, which I describe later in this chapter).

- It can also be difficult to buy shares in international companies from Australia, further limiting the scope for diversity. (Australia's sharemarket represents only about 2 per cent of total world sharemarkets.)

Different asset classes over time

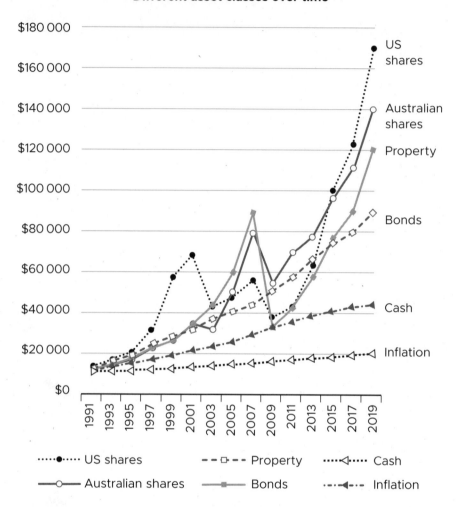

Note: This chart is just an approximation based on two-year intervals, while the sharemarket updates daily. The numbers provided are courtesy of Vanguard.

What shares to buy

When buying shares directly, there are well-established guidelines that you should follow (the principles also apply to managed funds, although in those cases the fund manager will take care of following many of these guidelines for you):

- **The golden rule of share investment as part of an investment strategy is to focus on 'blue chip' shares.** These are typically large, well-established companies that we know will be around for a long time and that will, despite the ups and downs of the market, provide regular, tax-advantaged income via dividends, in all but the most exceptional circumstances.

- **Keep investment in unusual or speculative shares to no more than 10 per cent of your portfolio.** It's fine to invest in that great tip you got from your mate at work, as long as you do your research and limit your investment, and you're comfortable with the risk. Speculative buys like this, whether they're in technology, or mining or any other industry, need to be understood as high risk. It's best to see them as a gamble—and as money you are prepared to lose.

- **Invest in a range of companies.** Diversify your investing into different companies, and certainly more than one—no matter how blue chip it is.

- **At the same time, don't invest in too many companies.** A good rule of thumb with blue chip shares is to invest no less than $10 000 in each company, and to invest in no more than 10 or 15 companies in total. If, say, you wanted to invest $100 000 in a share portfolio, you would be looking to invest in 10 different companies. This creates the opportunity to spread your investment across a range of industries, such as mining, banking, utilities, and so on. It is possible to make smaller investments—$5000 or even $2000 per company—allowing you to spread your funds across more businesses, but in my experience the management of 20, 30 or more small shareholdings can become a substantial administrative burden. And the returns are rarely worth the effort, as outperforming shares will usually be balanced by underperforming shares somewhere else. If you want maximum diversity, look at managed funds instead. Managed funds provide built-in diversity, as I discuss in the next section. Still, it is a good idea to spread your investment across a small number of different funds, say with varying risk profiles, rather than putting all your eggs in one basket.

Wrap accounts (where a flat fee covers all the administrative fees) can make the administration of investments across a range of shares and managed funds much easier.

Managed funds

Managed funds allow you to effectively own shares in a broad range of companies without having to buy into the individual companies themselves. Instead, a 'fund manager' pools your funds together with those of many other investors and then uses those funds to buy a broad range of shares—sometimes in hundreds of different companies. The value of your investment rises and falls with the value of the underlying shares owned by the fund.

Managed funds usually focus on a particular market sector, such as Australian shares, international shares or a diversified portfolio, with some aiming at narrower segments of these as well. Some funds deliberately aim for high levels of return on investment (in return for greater risk and/or volatility) while others are more conservative (providing generally lower returns but greater stability).

There are also managed funds that invest beyond shares and across a range of investment 'asset classes' such as property, commodities (such as gold), bonds and cash. These multi-asset funds are also known as 'mixed-asset' or 'diversified' funds[5] and are usually graded by their targeted level of return (from conservative to high growth—with accompanying levels of risk/volatility). To learn more about multi-asset funds and fund risk levels, see the later section 'Conservative, balanced, high growth: Aligning your risk profile to your investments'.

---

[5] There are no standard names for fund types, so you will find they vary widely—a consequence of marketing departments wanting their products to stand out. You may need to read the fine print to work out whether any particular fund invests in just a single class (for example, shares or property) or across a range of classes.

In addition to this categorisation, there are two main types of managed fund:

- **Index funds** aim to track market indices and as such are passive investments. A well-known example of an index is the S&P/ASX 200, which tracks the 200 largest companies on the Australian stock exchange. Numerous indices track a range of sectors by industry, company location (for example, Australian or international), risk level (for example, high growth, balanced or conservative) as well as more specialist categories. Fund managers such as Vanguard, who are probably the most well-known, aim to buy and sell shares to keep the fund in line with the 'benchmark' of the target index.

- **Active funds** are those in which the fund manager 'actively' tries to outperform the market index that the fund sets as a benchmark. They do this by selectively buying and selling shares based on analysis. Active fund managers use their expertise and ongoing management to change their funds' holdings, based on the financial conditions. A great example of this are multi-asset funds in which the majority of people are invested, especially the default 'Balanced' multi-asset fund of most employer superannuation funds.

Which are better — index funds or active funds?

There is an ongoing argument within the investment industry about the relative pros and cons of index funds and active funds. The reality is that both have their advantages and disadvantages. Traditionally, index funds were associated with lower management fees. If the sharemarket was trending upward, both types of fund would do well, so that fee difference gave index funds an advantage. On the other hand, active funds have traditionally performed better when the market was down or flat, as the expertise of the funds' managers squeezed better returns out of those conditions.

(continued)

Since 2010, index funds have done well. However, in recent years administration and investment fees have fallen across the board and this has led to a resurgence in the popularity of active funds. This has been helped by improved access to international stocks, which has given fund managers more options. Index funds for Australian shares have been dominated by only a few major companies, including the four banks, Telstra and BHP, so they are not as diverse as funds that invest in overseas sharemarkets.

Advantages of managed funds:

- They provide access to far greater diversity than most investors would be able to achieve by direct share investment.

- You are effectively tapping into the knowledge of professional investors and their research, which will nearly always, over time, outperform what you could do on your own.

- Administration is significantly reduced, as the fund provides a single annual statement summarising your income, with tax details. All other administrative matters are dealt with behind the scenes.

- They provide easier access to international shares.

- They can support small ongoing contributions more readily than other investment options.

Disadvantages of managed funds:

- Fund managers charge a fee for their services, which is deducted from your investment returns. This lowers the overall return on investment compared with owning direct shares. That said, management fees have come down significantly in recent years and generally range between 0.15 and 0.7 per cent per annum. (Index funds traditionally have had lower fees than active funds.)

- As an individual, selling units in a managed fund is not always as straightforward as selling shares.

- Some managed funds, depending on the nature of their underlying investments, can be exposed to less obvious risks such as fluctuations in the currency market or liquidity constraints that could make selling units difficult.

Investment platforms

Investment platforms provide a way to further diversify your investments while streamlining both investing and administration. They can be used for investments both inside and outside superannuation. Creating an account with an investment platform enables you to invest into, typically, a combination of direct shares, one or more managed funds, and other investments from within that single account. For a fee, the platform manages all the paperwork for you, providing (usually) online access to all your investments in one place, and a single annual statement at the end of each financial year for tax purposes.

Investment platforms are by far the most utilised share investing tool and are my preferred option for my clients.

Investment platforms used to be called 'master trusts' and only provided access to managed funds. The introduction of so-called 'wrap accounts' saw the offerings expand and become more sophisticated. Wrap accounts now offer access to managed funds, exchange-traded funds (ETFs; for more on these, see the later section 'Exchange-traded funds'), shares and other forms of investment all in one via a single platform and with greater reporting ability.

Separately managed accounts (SMAs) have recently emerged as another managed fund type. These distinguish themselves from other investment platforms in that they offer you the ability to directly own the underlying shares in your account. (In most other investment funds, the fund itself owns the underlying investments and you are buying units in the fund.) SMAs can provide more control and potential tax benefits; however, they are more complex arrangements.

Overall, investment platforms provide a much easier way of owning individual shares or units in managed funds, without the administration. The fees have in recent years become a fraction of what they were 10 years ago and so they're very cost effective as well as efficient. This is the preferred way for most investors, especially as for some platforms (wrap accounts) the investment choice is in the hundreds to choose from.

Financial advisers prefer investment platforms for ease of administration and the range of choice they can offer their clients. Examples of platforms we have used are Macquarie, Praemium and Netwealth. There are some excellent industry funds but usually they prefer their own in-house advisers. However, there are many others to choose from, with varying levels of sophistication, investment choices and fee structures, many of which are available for direct investment by individuals.

Advantages of investment platforms:

- They allow for a high level of diversity without the administrative burden.

- They simplify moving between investments.

- They often provide the ability to invest directly in international shares and managed funds.

- They can provide access to wholesale managed funds, which are normally only available to institutional investors and which often charge lower fees than their retail equivalents.

- They usually support the inclusion of other investment classes into your portfolio, such as fixed-interest bonds and property.

Disadvantages of investment platforms:

- They charge administration fees in addition to the investment fees associated with individual managed funds; they may charge other fees as well, such as for contributions, withdrawals and reporting.

- They usually offer investments in their own managed funds, so exiting a platform to change to a separate platform could be difficult.

Conservative, balanced, high growth: Aligning your risk profile to your investments

In Chapter 3, when you assessed your risk profile, you may remember the categories ranged from 'conservative' (low comfort with risk) through 'balanced' and up to 'high growth' (higher comfort with risk). I made reference to similar terminology when discussing multi-asset managed funds.

You may have noticed similar terminology on bank and investment websites or, most likely, on your annual superannuation statement. What do these terms mean in this context, and why should you care?

This has particular relevance to superannuation.

First, you need to understand that the money that goes into your superannuation fund is invested on your behalf into a managed fund. Like investment companies, all super funds have a range of managed funds to choose from, including a range of 'multi-asset' (or diversified) funds. Again, as with managed funds outside super, these multi-asset funds are graded in terms of risk/return, from 'conservative' at one end, through 'balanced' and up to 'high growth'.

Somewhere in your account you should be able to see which fund or funds your superannuation savings are currently invested in.

In most cases, the multi-asset managed fund your money goes into by default is the so-called 'balanced' fund.

This table provides an example of what the portfolios of a typical range of multi-asset funds might look like.

	Long term multi-asset mix			
	Growth %	Defensive %	Time frame	Description
Conservative	20	80	1–2 years	For investors who mainly want preservation of fixed assets (cash, fixed incomes, bonds etc.).
Moderately conservative	30	70	2–4 years	For investors who want a more diverse mix of assets, however still being cautious.
Balanced	50	50	4–6 years	For investors who want a balanced level of security and growth.
Growth	70	30	6–9 years	For investors who are willing to invest more in growth assets and have the possibility of a higher investment return for greater risk or volatility.
High-growth	90	10	+10 years	For investors who are more knowledgeable in their investing, relying on high-growth assets to potentially provide larger returns in the long term.

Take the time to try and understand this table and its implications. With a better understanding, you will be surprised how easy it is to ensure you know where your funds are now invested and what you may need to change for the future.

Why all the options?

Investment companies and superannuation funds create a range of these multi-asset funds to satisfy the various risk profiles of different investors. They modify the 'risk/growth' profiles of these funds through the choices they make about which shares and other assets they buy.

For instance, a more conservative fund will have a portfolio built largely on so-called 'defensive' assets, including cash and bonds.

In contrast, a high growth fund will have a portfolio weighted towards more volatile (but higher return over time) so-called 'growth' assets, such as shares (local and international), commodities and property.

In practice, most funds include some defensive assets and some growth assets. What differs is the proportions of these.

Balanced ain't always balanced

The 'balanced' fund is the default choice for most superannuation funds. As most Australians take a 'set and forget' approach to their super, balanced funds account for over 80 per cent of all super-annuation investments in this country. In addition, there's something psychologically satisfying about balanced funds sitting midway between the extremes of conservative and high growth.

Balanced funds were chosen as the default fund for superannuation investments as they were seen as balancing, as the name suggests, moderate risk with moderate returns. There is no firm definition of a balanced fund: each super fund defines the term as it sees fit.

Over the past decade or so, some balanced funds have sought to take advantage of a surging sharemarket by moving the goalposts. In some super funds, 'balanced' now means 60 per cent investment in growth assets, particularly shares, and 40 per cent in defensive assets. Some are even more aggressive, at as much as 80 per cent growth and 20 per cent defensive. That doesn't sound very balanced anymore, does it?

I don't have an issue with the higher returns this trend has provided for investors. However, I do have concerns with a lack of transparency.

Most fund members would have no idea that this change has taken place and that their 'balanced' investment is more volatile than it used to be.

The problem arises when the sharemarket, as it inevitably does, 'corrects' itself with a significant fall. This is precisely what happened when the market crashed in early 2020. The resultant fall in the value of many so-called balanced funds was far greater than many investors expected.

What does this mean for you? Again it comes down to knowledge. You may be happy with your superannuation in a balanced fund with a higher percentage in growth assets and potential returns. Just double check your fund's website to satisfy yourself how it is actually invested.

The Goldilocks phenomenon — why 'high growth' may be a better option

Whether you have chosen it or it's the 'default' fund, many working Australians are in the Balanced fund of their superannuation plan. Staying in 'balanced' may feel more comfortable (as with Goldilocks, not too aggressive and not too conservative), though it could mean that you are missing out on significant investment returns. In practice, according to research by Vanguard, 'high growth' funds typically generate returns of around 2 to 3 per cent per annum higher, on average, than balanced funds over the longer term, as a higher share component.

If that doesn't sound like much, consider this: on a $120 000 super balance, an assumed extra 2.5 per cent year on year would generate over $50 000 in additional interest over a decade. After 30 years — the typical period over which most people's super is invested — your account balance would be more than double what it would otherwise be. To see what I mean, consider the trend in this chart.

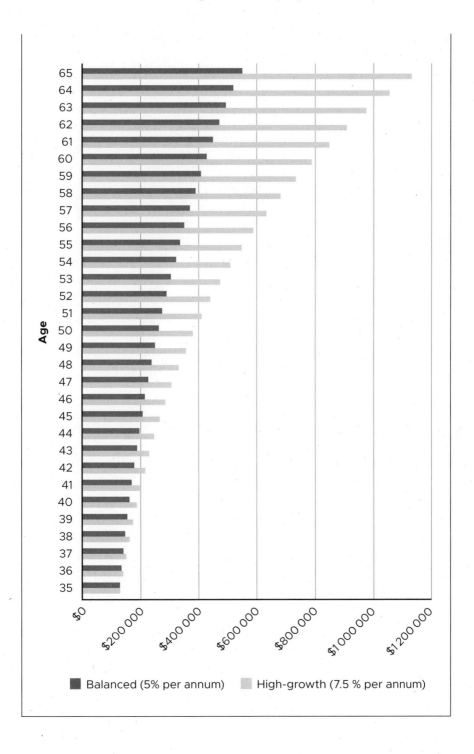

Why investing only in Australian shares is not always best

Another psychological factor at play in many investment decisions is *domestic bias*. This is another way of saying that 'you invest in what you know'. Most people are more comfortable buying an investment property in their local area, as they understand what's happening in that area. The same psychology extends to shares. In Australia, we all know about the 'big four' banks, Telstra, BHP, and so on, so it's understandable that we tend to invest in these companies. The same applies to institutional investors such as super funds.

While I would never say you shouldn't invest in good-quality Australian stocks, there are two reasons why you should at least consider what is happening in the rest of the world when you are building your investment strategy.

First, the Australian sharemarket accounts for less than 2 per cent of global sharemarkets and is dominated by just 10 companies, plus the big four banks, so it's not particularly diversified.

Second, other markets may have better opportunities. At the time of the Global Financial Crisis in 2008, the ASX 200 index had just broken through the 6000 level for the first time while the USA's Dow Jones was at 16 000. In late 2020, the ASX 200 was just over 7000 compared to the Dow Jones, which was closer to 30 000.

You can access international shares via global managed funds — such as Morningstar, Russell and Vanguard to name a few — which are offered by all the major investment and super companies. Check the underlying investments of your managed multi-asset fund and if it is too highly weighted towards Australian shares, it may well be worth considering topping up your investment with a 5 to 10 per cent investment in a small range of global equity funds via an investment platform. This will provide further diversity to your portfolio.

When to buy shares or invest in managed funds

It makes sense that the best time to be buying shares or units in managed funds is after the market has fallen. When you start to see the headlines that the market has crashed and the world is ending, that it's a catastrophe, that everyone is losing everything, that's the time when the 'smart' investors are buying.

I liken it to Christmas sale time, when the shoes that were valued at $200 one day are suddenly valued at half that price the next day.

The shoes haven't changed—it's just that their price has dropped. In a similar way, the BHP or Telstra shares, or units in a managed fund, you buy in the days after the market falls, at 10 or 20 per cent lower than their typical price: they're just the same shares or units, only cheaper.

Just like the shoes, though, the golden rule applies. The best shares to buy in a 'sale' period are those in blue chip companies that you know will be around, continuing to pay dividends, for the long term.

Dollar cost averaging

Of course, you can't always wait for a sharemarket crash to get into the market. Significant 'corrections', as they are called euphemistically, occur roughly once per decade, which is a long time to wait for a sale.

Most of the time you would look to invest during 'normal' times when the market is neither highly overheated nor significantly depressed. A good strategy for buying shares (or units in managed funds) in 'normal' times is so-called 'dollar cost averaging'. The way this works is that if, say, you have $12 000 to invest in a given share, you buy $1000 worth of that share every month for 12 months. This evens out any impact of the fundamentally unpredictable ups and downs of the market during that period.

Dollar cost averaging won't lead to you buying at the lowest possible price over that 12-month period, but it won't mean you end up buying at the highest price either. To do otherwise—to 'pick the market' and buy at rock bottom—would require a crystal ball and is not a wise strategy with any investment. At the same time, it does give you the flexibility to take advantage of a market correction should one occur over that period.

Borrowing to buy shares

You can leverage the potential benefits of investing in shares or managed funds by borrowing funds to invest. However, this sort of investment comes with various caveats due to the volatility of the sharemarkets. When it comes to shares, leverage works both ways: just as it can help you amplify returns from share investments, it has the potential to also amplify losses. That being the case, borrowing to buy shares needs to be consistent with your investment strategy and your risk profile.

The most common way to borrow for share investments is to use equity in a property, such as your home, as the collateral. This provides both you and the bank with a more secure backing for the loan, making it fundamentally more stable.

Borrowing against your home will usually be something you can do as either a redraw, if you have a current loan or line of credit in place, or a separate investment loan backed by your property. In the current low-interest market, these loans cost in the range 3 to 5 per cent per annum. Historically, good-quality shares held for over 10 years have consistently earned returns in excess of this when both capital growth and dividend income are taken into account.

An advantage of using a redraw facility is that you don't need to justify your actions to the bank. As they already hold the mortgage on your home as collateral, they're not particularly interested in whether you are spending redrawn funds on a holiday, renovations or some sort of investment.

That's not to say that you should be taking unnecessary risks. When borrowing against your home it pays to be more conservative than you might otherwise be. The last thing you want to do is put your home at risk. Some general rules of thumb when borrowing in this way:

- Borrow no more than half of what you can afford to borrow.

- Borrow no more than 20 per cent of the value of your home.

- Borrow only for more conservative share investments—for example, blue chip stocks—and not for speculative buys. Don't gamble with your home.

- Follow all the other guidelines described in this chapter.

Though I don't often recommend the use of the family home as collateral for a share investment loan, I often strike resistance from our clients when we do so. There seems to be something psychological about this because the same people can be quite comfortable borrowing against their home to fund an investment property. Perhaps it is the media's obsession with the rises and falls in the sharemarket that paints a picture of volatility you don't see in property.

If we focus on the facts, the reality is that over the long term, sharemarkets have consistently provided stronger returns on investment than property, so investing in shares is often a sounder investment strategy. That said, including both property and shares in your investment portfolio adds diversity and makes sound sense.

And to reiterate: the information and advice in this book is general in nature. Before making any substantial decisions that might affect your livelihood or financial position or put your home at risk, you should consider seeking professional advice and a second opinion.

Tax and shares

While many tax considerations apply equally to all investment types, there are particular aspects of tax as it applies to share ownership that have implications for tax planning. It's not the place of this book to get into these in great detail, but let's look at the basics.

Franking credits

When you receive a dividend statement for a company you own shares in, the statement may include various numbers referring to 'franking credits'. This is a complex topic, but the underlying concept is fairly straightforward.

Dividend income you receive from a company you own shares in is generally taxable at your *marginal tax rate*; that is, the highest rate of tax you are paying based on your total taxable income.

Without going into the mechanics of it, *franking credits* provide the opportunity to claim back tax already paid by the company paying the dividend.

For this purpose, the number that matters on your dividend statement will be labelled as the 'franking credit' or 'Australian franking credit'. This amount can be applied as a deduction to your tax return, helping to reduce your taxable income tax or potentially earning you a tax refund.

Capital gains tax

Capital gains tax (CGT) is only relevant when you sell. Assuming the shares are worth more than you paid for them, any 'profit' you make from the sale price (being higher than what you originally paid for them) will be taxable at your marginal tax rate. There are a couple of variations to this:

- Provided you have held the shares for over 12 months, a CGT discount of 50 per cent applies. That is, you will only owe tax on half the capital gain.

- If you sell shares at a loss, that loss can be offset against other capital gains. So if, for instance, you lost $1000 on one share sale and made $1500 on another, your net capital gain would be $500 (before application of any CGT discount). Losses can be carried forward and deducted against future gains.

Note that capital gains tax applies to all capital assets (with some exemptions)—not just shares. Two main exemptions are the family home and assets purchased before 20 September 1985.

The benefits of having a good accountant

As with any professional adviser you have—your doctor, your financial adviser, your lawyer—not all accountants are the same. Sometimes you need to shop around to find the one that suits you best. Once you start building assets and your affairs become more complex, getting the best advice to minimise your tax is essential.

At this point, finding the right accountant to build a long-term relationship with becomes very important. Ideally, your accountant and financial adviser should work together on your behalf. Your lawyer should be included in this team as well when it comes to your estate planning.

Property as an investment

For most members of the sandwich generation, property ownership has always meant, first and foremost, owning their own home. It's the Australian way. Their children, the millennials, are also interested in property, but with a different focus. They see property in terms of its investment potential. There are a number of reasons for that, often including living and working overseas, and I return to the perspective of millennials in Chapter 8.

The point I want to make here is that the millennials are onto something; that is, the real potential benefits of property investment. Property investment can be a valuable component of a 'financial freedom' investment strategy, particularly when that strategy is focused on income over capital growth.

Options for buying property

As with shares, there are various different ways you can get into the property market. Property has a number of potential benefits over other investments, including:

- **Property is a tangible asset with a generally stable value.** While property prices can rise (and fall) over time, this rarely happens significantly in the short term, while in the longer term they will generally trend upwards. Property values are certainly less volatile than those of shares.

- **Investment property can provide a steady stream of income.** This income can then offset most or all of the costs of owning the property, including interest and maintenance costs.

- **Property investment in the current climate provides various tax advantages.** One example is the protection of negative gearing (see the later section 'Tax and property investments); another tax advantage is discounted capital gains tax.

Purchasing a property directly

The most obvious way to get into the investment property market is to buy a property in your own name: an apartment, a holiday house, a suburban house or even a commercial property. Choosing an appropriate property is the topic for another book entirely (and there have been plenty written already). Suffice to say there are some golden rules that you need to follow.

Here are my golden rules:

1. **Location, location, location.** It's an old saying but still very true. Get to know the demographics of any area you are interested in before you start. Is it a growing area? Is there a new hospital or Bunnings being built—anything to show signs of growth in the area? Something I like to check is whether there is a McDonald's close by. The company spends millions on research for growth

trends before setting up a new restaurant. You can piggyback off their hard work!

2. **Follow the money.** It's not about how much a property is worth now; it's more about how much its value is likely to grow (capital gain) in the coming years and how much income (via rent) it could provide. That's why another real estate truism is: 'Don't buy the best house in the street.' The worst house in a good area has the most potential to grow.

3. **Take the emotion out of it.** When making any sound property investment decision, think with a clear and focused mind rather than making it an emotional choice, taking a punt or speculating. It's too big a purchase to gamble on, so have a plan. (This point is just as valid for other investments as it is for property.)

4. **Property is like shares: the market goes in cycles, so do the research.** See whether the area you are interested in is at the top of the market or bottom, or somewhere in between. Your view on this will likely be different for an investment property as opposed to buying a home to live in. In the latter case, you may have a longer-term perspective and can wait until the market starts to move up, as good property usually does over time.

5. **Cover your bases first.** Before bidding on or getting serious about a specific property, make sure you have done your homework. Work out what level of deposit you have or need, what your buying limit is, and what your mortgage and the associated repayments would be. Other considerations include whether you are financing the loan on one salary or two (and, if two, what would happen if you dropped down to just one salary), and whether you have insurance and a proper safety net in place.

6. **Get advice.** Whether it is from your bank, mortgage broker, financial adviser, property advocates, friends or even Google, learn as much as you can about property before you dive in. While good properties tend to increase in value over time, there are plenty of horror stories of people buying the wrong property and watching its value fall away.

Advantages of direct purchase:

- You can choose an investment property that will suit your needs, such as a place you might want to live in yourself in future.

- You have direct control over your investment.

- Property can provide solid income through rental payments.

Disadvantages of direct purchase:

- Property requires hands-on management (though this can be outsourced to a property manager).

- Returns will drop if the property sits vacant for a sustained period.

- Property can be difficult to liquidate (sell), depending on the overall state of the real estate market at the time.

Using a property advocate

If you have been through the process of buying a property, whether as your own home or as an investment, you know it takes many weekends and endless research looking through umpteen properties to find the right one. Then, on auction day, there always seems to be that person who has endless money, so after all that work you miss out on the dream property and have to start all over again. It's very frustrating.

In recent years, property advocates have become very popular. These are people, usually with a real estate background, who do the legwork for you, including searching for properties based on your specifications and then negotiating the price for you. They will even bid on your behalf at auction if necessary (with the advantage of being more experienced at the process and without the emotion you would bring to it). This rising popularity is in part due to most people simply not having the time to do the work needed, but also recognition that advocates have much better knowledge of the market (they spend all their time in it). They also often have access to 'off-market' opportunities rarely available to the general public.

Using a property advocate can be a highly worthwhile exercise, especially if you are planning to buy an investment property.

Property advocates are not cheap. In my experience, average fees are in the range $15 000 to $25 000. However, they can usually negotiate a final price that will save you that amount regardless. Given the property purchase itself will likely be at least $700 000—a very significant investment—it simply makes sense to have someone working on your behalf who understands the market and knows what mistakes to avoid. Making the wrong decision would cost you far more than the advocate's fee.

If you want to buy a property in your own area, an area you understand well and know the nuances of, perhaps the use of an advocate would be unnecessary. However, even then, property advocates can provide knowledge and expertise that you simply cannot accrue yourself, as well as taking the emotion out of the purchase. And you can have your weekends back.

As with financial advisers, the best strategy when choosing a property advocate is to meet a few, see what they can do for you and find one you feel comfortable working with.

Investing in property trusts

Another way to invest in property without having to actually buy and manage an individual property is via a *property trust*. These are entities that own and manage a portfolio of properties, typically commercial properties. The funds you invest with the trust are combined with those of others for the purchase of properties, the capital value of your investment will rise or fall with the value of the owned properties, and income is derived from rental payments and shared among the investors (less management fees).

Property trusts come in two forms: 'listed' and 'unlisted'.

- With an *unlisted trust*, you are effectively buying a direct share of the trust's property portfolio.

- With *listed trusts*, by contrast, you buy and sell units in the trust on the sharemarket, much as you would any other share or ETF. Buying and selling units in a listed trust is typically easier than doing so in an unlisted trust, but listed trusts are also subject to the volatility of the sharemarket as a whole.

Property trusts have a chequered history as investments. There have been various examples over the last few decades of trusts collapsing and leaving investors with large losses. Unfortunately, these always come with stories of people who have invested all their savings in the trust and been left with nothing.

For this reason, I urge you to use caution if looking at property trusts as investments. Only consider larger, well-established, well-backed trusts, and ensure such investments form only part of your well-diversified portfolio.

Advantages of property trusts:

- They provide access to the property sector with greater diversity than owning one, or a small number of, individual properties.

- They can provide access to areas of the property sector, such as commercial real estate, that are otherwise difficult to get into.

Disadvantages of property trusts:

- They can have constraints on liquidity, depending on the nature of the fund.

- Historically, poorly managed property trusts have been associated with some large, newsworthy collapses.

Diversifying in property with managed funds

Managed funds that focus on property—such as Charter Hall, Trilogy and Centuria for example—are a way of accessing property trusts while at the same time diversifying your investment. Managed funds in property offer similar advantages and disadvantages to their sharemarket counterparts.

Some investment platforms (refer to the earlier section 'Investment platforms') facilitate the incorporation of property investments, particularly via managed funds.

Borrowing for property investment

Funding a direct property purchase

If you are looking to directly buy an investment property, you will probably need to take out a loan to fund the purchase. Even if you have access to sufficient cash, it could be sensible to borrow to buy the property and put the cash into some other form of investment. This can be an effective way of using 'good debt' to your advantage.

As with a home loan, there are really two main ways of financing an investment property purchase: directly with a bank or via a *mortgage broker*.

Obtaining funding from a bank

Going direct to a bank, particularly one of the major four banks, can be worthwhile if they are providing a competitive interest rate and if you have been banking with them for a long time. If you have an existing or previous mortgage with them, and/or some credit card history, and/or you have savings with them, the bank's existing knowledge of you can streamline the process.

Using a mortgage broker

The property funding market is highly competitive today and so unless you are sure you are getting the best deal from your bank, it makes sense to consult a mortgage broker, who can quickly obtain three or four quotes.

Mortgage brokers can't always find better rates than the banks are offering, but they will be able to give you a good view of the options.

Building a relationship with a mortgage broker can have advantages in its own right. A mortgage broker is a small businessperson, and as such it is in their interest to get to know you and, hopefully, work with you over the longer term. (The bank was once like that too, back when you could visit and even get to know your local bank manager, but those days are now long gone.)

The best way of finding a mortgage broker is by word of mouth. Your financial adviser might be able to recommend someone—often someone they work with themselves—as might a friend who's had a good experience. If you can't get a referral, search for someone nearby and at least ask for references from them that you can check out.

Funding property trusts or managed fund investments

As with shares, you may be able to leverage the potential returns of property trusts and managed funds in the property sector through the use of borrowed funds. This approach comes with the same caveats as borrowing to invest in shares. Although the property market is generally not as volatile as the sharemarket, it does have risks associated with it. As with shares, borrowing to invest in property needs to be consistent with your investment strategy and your risk profile.

For most in the sandwich generation, the simplest way to access funds for investing in this way is to use equity in a property you already own, such as your own home. My guidelines for this are the same as for using borrowed money to buy shares—refer to the earlier section 'Borrowing to buy shares'.

Tax and property investments

As with shares, various tax rules apply to property investments. Capital gains tax (CGT) applies to property investments in the same way as it does to shares (refer to the earlier section 'Tax and shares' for more information) and other capital assets. But as with shares, CGT is only relevant at the time you sell a property.

The most relevant tax rules to direct property investment are those around so-called 'negative gearing'.

Negative gearing (which is not an official term) refers to the tax rules that allow an investor to claim as a tax deduction any losses associated with the cost of owning an investment property.

Negative gearing is quite simple in principle. An investment property (hopefully) earns revenue in the form of rent. Owning that property also incurs costs in the form of things like interest payments, maintenance and property management. If those costs exceed the revenue, the loss (the negative) can be claimed as a tax deduction against your other sources of income.

A secondary advantage of negative gearing is that you can minimise the cost of owning an investment property while continuing to benefit from its capital growth.

There is a point to make here about the tax aspect of this. While negative gearing can be used as a legitimate part of a strategy for tax minimisation, it should not be seen as a form of tax avoidance. By that I mean that if circumstances are such that your rental income exceeds the costs of owning your property—that is, you are 'positively geared'—you will need to pay tax on that excess income. While some people baulk at the idea of paying tax in this way, it needs to be remembered that it is a good sign. If you are paying tax, it means you are earning more money than you would be if you had a loss to offset, and that's usually a good thing!

This point is particularly relevant in a low inflation, low interest rate environment. For much of the last 30 years, negative gearing has been a central focus of property investors, and they were able to achieve this because interest rates were high relative to rental income.

Today, astute investment choices with strong rental income, even where that is at the expense of negative gearing, are becoming more popular.

Note that the tax deductibility of investment losses (that is, negative gearing) applies to all investments, including shares. However, in practice its application is most common in property.

Other investment options

While shares and property are the 'all stars' of the investment world, there are other options that can be used to add breadth and diversity to your investment portfolio. While I have provided some of the more popular options, the list of possibilities is endless. The following sections describe a few of the readily available options. There are many others, including LICs (listed investment companies), REITs (real estate investment trusts) and emerging areas such as 'peer to peer', all of which a financial adviser could talk you through.

Exchange-traded funds

An *exchange-traded fund* or ETF is a special form of managed fund, the units of which are traded on the stock exchange in the same way that shares are bought and sold. In other words, you can buy and sell units in ETFs using the same online brokerage account that you would use for buying and selling shares in individual companies.

ETFs are available across a range of market segments, with the main benefit being lower fee costs than the traditional managed funds that they are based on.

Term deposits and 'bonus saver' accounts

Today's transaction accounts typically pay zero interest, or so little that it might as well be zero. However, higher interest is usually available from your bank through term deposits and, often, so-called 'bonus saver' accounts.

Term deposits provide a pre-defined interest rate over the fixed term of your deposit, after which you'll have the choice to withdraw the funds or roll them over into a new fixed term. Interest rates available vary with the time you are willing to lock away your funds, the rates dependent to some extent on where the bank's analysts see interest rates moving over the short to medium term.

Bonus saver accounts (the names vary with marketers' tastes) provide a higher rate of interest than rock-bottom transaction accounts for any month in which you don't make any withdrawals. Popular examples of these types of accounts are Macquarie Bank's high interest savings account, ING's Savings Maximiser savings account and Rabobank's high interest savings account.

Bank accounts—even those offering slightly higher interest—are not viable as long-term investment options unless you have an extremely low risk profile. However, they can provide flexibility in the short term so might form part of an overall investment strategy.

All bank account interest is taxable at your marginal rate.

Insurance bonds

Insurance bonds, also called *investment bonds*, are a relatively little-known form of investment that can provide long-term tax benefits. Insurance bonds are offered by some life insurance companies (such as Generation Life, CommBank and Centuria) and friendly societies, which invest the funds raised on behalf of the bond holders. They generally pay interest similar to any managed funds with similar types of underlying investment choices (catering to a range of risk profiles and tolerances), and that interest is tax free effectively, the tax having been paid by the insurance company over the life of the investment. (The company tax rate, currently 30 per cent, will be reflected in the returns of these investments.)

Insurance bonds are also free of capital gains tax on withdrawal as long as they are held for 10 years or more, though even if you needed to cash in your bond within that time there are still significant tax savings available.

Insurance bonds can be a good tax-effective long-term investment, particularly for those on high incomes or who have reached the cap on contributions to their superannuation (which I discuss in Chapter 5). Many enjoy the benefits of these investment vehicles by using them to create a savings plan upon the birth of their children, which will ultimately, with the help of compounding interest, be used to pay for the children's secondary school fees.

Fixed-interest bonds

Generally accessed through managed funds, *fixed-interest bonds*—which governments and corporations use to raise funds—can provide low-volatility investment options that nevertheless generally provide better returns than most bank accounts. Tax is payable on any interest payments made from these funds, at your marginal rate.

Gold

For most of the investment options described so far, I have provided general information, including advantages and disadvantages. Gold is a different type of investment, as much because of its emotional appeal as anything else. Gold as an investment splits the investment community.

While it is no longer the 'standard' by which governments value their currencies, governments continue to hold gold as a buffer against downturns in the sharemarket. When the market does fall, you will nearly always be able to find news stories encouraging the buying of gold. It is a highly tangible investment, after all. And of course it will always have high value for jewellery.

All that being said, the fact is that the sharemarket has outperformed gold by 4 to 1 in the last 10+ years. More importantly, it breaks my rule that a good asset should always provide an income stream. Gold doesn't do that.

Cryptocurrencies

I have no experience with cryptocurrencies and I imagine most in the sandwich generation share that lack of experience. I include them in this list only because we have all seen or read many articles on cryptocurrencies (the best known of which is Bitcoin) as 'the next big thing'. For those who don't know, a *cryptocurrency* is a 'virtual' currency as it has no physical representation in the form of coins or notes.

My view is that as cryptocurrencies are not legal tender, nor backed by any government, you should be cautious. If you are going to invest in any high-risk or speculative investment, limit your investment to what you can afford to lose (no more than 10 per cent of your portfolio).

Your action plan and next steps

☐ Once you feel comfortable with investing and the different asset classes, review your existing investments and superannuation to see if they could be reorganised for better potential growth or income.

☐ If your savings plans are for the long term but you are invested in short-term accounts like term deposits, it's time to review your investment strategy and possibly consider shares as an option.

☐ For all investing, make sure you diversify across different assets.

☐ If property investment is a goal, whether for a home or an investment, make sure you follow the guidelines set out in this book.

In Chapter 10, I share a full 12-month action plan incorporating many of these actions. In addition, my website (themoneysandwich.com) has plenty of templates, calculators and general information to help you with this process.

5

Optimising your superannuation

What's in this chapter

Plan ahead

'Year R': The big questions

Superannuation: The basics

Super: The tax haven everyone can use

Superannuation myths

Taking control of your superannuation investment

Investment strategies for superannuation

New Zealand's retirement system

Some final words on superannuation

The idea of an investment plan and strategy and the various investment options available, as discussed in Chapter 4, is relevant at any stage of your life. The strategy might change with your circumstances or stage of life, but the need to have a strategy doesn't.

In this chapter, we focus on preparing for 'Year R' specifically in terms of your superannuation, and on managing your superannuation beyond Year R. Australia's superannuation system provides a number of advantages, particularly around the taxing of super contributions and earnings, that are designed to make superannuation an attractive proposition.

The big points: Your post-work financial strategy

What you can do right now, no questions asked

1. Write a paragraph (or more) that describes the way you see your lifestyle after 'Year R'; that is, after you move into what for most people are the 'post-work' years. This is not just your Year R goals that you set out in Chapter 3 (such as retiring comfortably), which are more financial. This is about what your next challenge will be, what you would like to do with all this new free time you have on your hands. See the later section 'Year R: The big questions' for more on this.

2. Invest some time to get a basic understanding of the way superannuation works and the tax advantages available via superannuation, especially once you turn 60. Read through this chapter carefully. Look through the pages relevant to superannuation on the Australian Taxation Office (ATO) website (search 'super') or the ASIC Moneysmart website (search for 'plan for the future'). Even if you have no interest in this topic, it would serve you well to spend some time getting an overview

3. Get access to your account on your superannuation fund's website. Familiarise yourself with what savings you currently have in that account and what multi-asset investment (for example, conservative/balanced/growth/high growth) your money is allocated to.

4. If married or in a long-term relationship, make sure you and your partner are both aware of what your superannuation entitlements are. The limits on superannuation generally apply to individuals, which in practice means that couples can access double the benefits between them. I discuss this in more detail in this chapter.

5. Find out how much you are paying in fees to your superannuation fund every year. (You'll find this information on the fund's website, often inside the downloadable Product Disclosure Statement or PDS.) There are plenty of low-cost super fund options, and if you have been with the same fund for 10 years or longer, there's a good chance you are paying higher fees than you need to.

Plan ahead

While people in their 50s may not see the age of 65 as a firmly drawn line in the sand, the reality is that Australian governments, through the superannuation and pension system, still see the age of 65 as a 'standard' retirement age. This has a range of implications, many of which we will discuss. (You might be interested to know that the link between the age of 65 and the pension was first introduced by the Australian government in 1908. Back then, the average life expectancy was 55, so most weren't expected to receive a pension, whereas life expectancy is now in the 80s.)

The point to make at the outset is that to take best advantage of the benefits of the superannuation system after the age of 65, you need to be planning as far ahead as you can—preferably a decade at least. That makes this chapter particularly important for you if you are currently in your 50s but have not yet given much thought to a superannuation strategy.

Don't throw out your investment strategy when you retire

Stopping paid work and no longer contributing to your super doesn't mean disregarding your risk profile or previous investment strategy. There is a strong implication in the advertising aimed at retirees that stopping work means you should 'go conservative', hunker down and safeguard your superannuation balance from any future market volatility. However, as it's quite possible you will live another 30 years or so, you need your super and other assets to last as long as possible—and that means they need to do their part in earning their keep. Even if there is a market downturn once every decade, there is a high likelihood the sharemarket will continue to outperform most other investments over that 30-year period.

So certainly review your risk profile, and perhaps bring it down a notch if that makes you more comfortable or you have enough assets, but don't ignore your investment strategy altogether when you retire. Similarly, talk to your financial adviser about how your investment strategy might change post-Year R.

'Year R': The big questions

Many people look towards retirement from a purely financial perspective. This is understandable in that getting your finances right is a very important part of preparing for Year R. However, it is only one part. You also need to be prepared for retirement emotionally and physically, including answering the biggest question: 'What will you do once retired?'

Let's summarise the main factors at play as you approach Year R.

Lifestyle considerations

If you had no constraints, financial or otherwise, what would you do once you reach retirement age? Would you:

- take a traditional retirement, then spend your time on recreational activities and whatever else you choose, but mainly around your home?

- continue to work more-or-less as you are now, because you enjoy your work and believe you still have a few years of contribution left to make? Perhaps your ideal is to gradually reduce your hours, or shift to a slightly less hands-on role?

- take the opportunity to pursue another line of work, one that is a real passion? Perhaps this might involve going into business for yourself, turning that hobby into something that will bring in some income? Perhaps it will have a voluntary component?

- stop work but also make a significant shift in your lifestyle, such as spending six months of each year travelling, or downsizing the house, buying a caravan and travelling indefinitely?

There is no shortage of options. I know people who are keen to finish work as soon as they can so they can turn their attention to a cause they are dedicated to, while I also know people in their 80s who are still working full-time, love what they do and have no intention of stopping.

Of course you may not have the luxury of complete freedom in choosing your direction, but don't concern yourself with that for the moment. We're not thinking financial, we're thinking dreams here.

Thinking about future lifestyle considerations is even more important for couples, who in my experience often have differing perspectives of what the future might look like but haven't necessarily found the time to discuss those perspectives with each other in order to agree on a shared direction.

Mental/emotional considerations

This topic is closely related to the previous one but is worth pondering separately. How much are you truly invested in the work you do now? What are you passionate about? Is there any overlap of your passion with your work? How much do you need something—some sort of work—to keep you engaged with life? How many games of golf would you be able to play before you became bored? Again, this is something that needs to be discussed with your partner.

Financial considerations

When you have a clearer idea of what you'd like the future to look like, it's easier to start planning. There are times when we have to have difficult conversations with people about their expectations and the reality of their finances. There are some who get to 65 and really want to retire but, for whatever reasons, they haven't been able to accrue enough assets to support the lifestyle they tell us they want. Sometimes that may mean continuing to work for a while. The unfortunate thing is that often, had these people only started their planning a bit earlier, even in their early to mid-50s, they might have been able to work their way into a better situation.

Hence my emphasis on planning ahead to build the wealth you'll need to achieve your post-Year R lifestyle goals. And superannuation planning is a big part of that.

The big questions

The big questions I'm flagging here are actually quite simple—though they may not be easy to answer. There are two overarching questions: 'What do you want to do in your post-Year R life?' and 'How long will you be able to keep doing that?' We can break each question down into two parts:

What do you want to do in your post-Year R life?

- **What's your next challenge?** You are entering a new phase of your life, and for it to be rewarding it has to provide you with a challenge. You would be amazed how quickly some people become bored in retirement or, even worse, feel their self-worth has diminished, especially if they have previously been defined by their work.

- **How will this fit in with your relationship?** Many couples have not spent a lot of time with each other in the 20 years or so before Year R—or not as much as they may think. Work-life and kids can do that to you! Your children leaving home can leave you unprepared for being with each other almost all the time. Looking after elderly parents may require you to allocate more time to their care and travel to do this. This can be a wonderful new stage of life, but again it is best discussed and thought about ahead of time.

How long will you be able to keep going?

- **What are you doing to maintain your health and wellbeing?** As we get older, most people seem to spend less and less time on their health and wellbeing. However, achieving the best quality of life you can for the next 30-odd years is worth putting the effort into. Once retired, you will have more time to spend on your health and wellbeing. (See Chapter 9 for more on this topic.)

- **What are you doing to ensure the money lasts?** Are your savings invested wisely and tax efficiently? Are you in control of your money, and in particular your spending? These things, of course, are the main reasons for reading this book!

Superannuation: The basics

Superannuation is a big deal—and big business—in Australia. Since employer superannuation contributions became compulsory—the 'Super Guarantee'—in the 1980s, Australians have collectively accrued (and drawn on) trillions of dollars' worth of superannuation assets. As of February 2020, the value of assets in superannuation accounts totalled $3 trillion.[6]

For most working Australians, their superannuation will be their second biggest asset after their home.

Unfortunately, very few people understand how superannuation operates, the rules around it, and how to optimise super contributions and, ultimately, payments, to suit their chosen lifestyle. However, particularly as you approach Year R, it is important to get your head around super generally, as well as your own super situation.

Before we start, a general statement/warning: superannuation is complex—it is nearly impossible to describe any aspect of it without adding some sort of rider like 'except when ...' or 'in certain cases ...'. Like tax, it is an area in which you really need to seek professional advice pertaining to your specific situation.

That said, here are the main things you need to understand about superannuation:

- **At its simplest, superannuation is a form of mandatory saving.** For most people, their superannuation savings are made up of employer contributions made before tax. In other words, you don't see the money: it goes straight from your employer to your super fund. It is possible to add further savings 'inside' superannuation, with various terms and conditions. (I'll use the terms 'inside super' and 'outside super' a few times in this chapter. Any money or investments inside super are said to be 'preserved' and are subject to the

---

[6]www.superannuation.asn.au/resources/superannuation-statistics.

pre-preservation age restrictions. Money and investments outside super are the opposite.)

- **Money contributed to a superannuation fund is invested on your behalf by that fund, usually across a range of shares, property, cash and other investments.**

- **The main distinguishing feature of superannuation is that the funds cannot be accessed until your 'preservation age', which for most people is age 60.** After that milestone, you can—and eventually must—start to withdraw your money from the fund with various conditions and restrictions. (Your preservation age is 60 years if you were born after 1 July 1964, but slightly lower for those born before that point.)

- **While you can't spend your superannuation savings until you reach your preservation age, you can move those savings between superannuation funds, between investments within a super fund or even into other forms of investment (with various restrictions).** This is where there are opportunities to be more creative with your super investments.

- **Superannuation is effectively the only legal tax haven available to the typical Australian salary earner (once retired).** There are various tax advantages associated with superannuation contributions and earnings. This becomes more important in the decade or so before Year R, as the actions you take in that decade will determine the extent to which you are able to take full advantage of the benefits the government makes available.

Governments, particularly Australian governments, actively encourage superannuation because it relieves pressure on the social security system. The more people whose retirement is funded by their superannuation, the fewer people who will be reliant on the government-funded pension. This appreciation for superannuation has been reflected over the years in the growth of the rate of the employer-contributed Super Guarantee from an initial 3 per cent of salary per annum to the current 10 per cent of salary per annum (and a planned increase to 12 per cent in the future).

How super works in practice

Superannuation is incredibly complex, and it only gets more so as each successive government finds reasons to tinker with it. That said, we can summarise some of the main points so that you have an overview of how superannuation works in practice. A warning, though: you might have to read this a few times before it starts to make sense! There's no shortage of jargon, including some, frankly, strange terminology used by the ATO. The accompanying diagram may help.

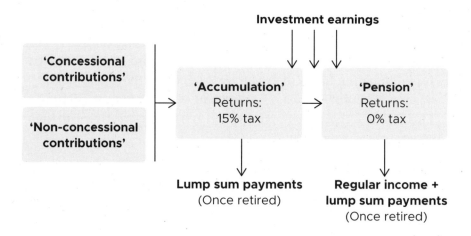

Getting money into super

Unless you have already moved past your preservation age, you may not be aware that superannuation has two official phases: the *accumulation phase* and the *pension (retirement[7]) phase*. Put simply, these represent the phases of adding to and withdrawing from your superannuation, respectively. In practice, accumulation and pension can overlap, but we'll come back to that.

---

[7] Since 2017, the 'pension phase' has officially been called the 'retirement phase'. However, as the terms 'pension phase' and 'pension account' are still used by most people, I'm using those terms in this book.

We'll start by looking at the accumulation phase: how you add funds to your superannuation.

The accumulation phase starts when you get your first job. Anyone who earns a wage, which is most people, started 'accumulating' superannuation from their first day of work. Funds—equivalent to (currently) 10 per cent of your gross salary—are added to a superannuation fund on your behalf by your employer under the Super Guarantee.

Employer contributions are the simple, set-and-forget part of super. Many people may not even be aware that this 'compulsory saving' is taking place.

Now it gets more complicated.

Aside from employer contributions, there are various other ways to build up—known as 'contributing to'—your superannuation. Contributions fall into two categories, depending on whether the contributions are made from your gross, pre-tax income—so-called *concessional contributions*—or your net, after-tax income, so-called *non-concessional contributions*.

Here are all the ways funds can be added to your super.

Concessional contributions

Concessional (pre-tax) contributions can be made up from:

- **Employer contributions:** Also known as 'Superannuation Guarantee Contributions' (SGC), these are currently set at 10 per cent on top of your gross salary.

- **Salary sacrifice contributions:** As an employee, you contribute an extra amount of your salary, pre-tax, into your super fund.

- **Personal after-tax contributions to your superannuation:** These contributions are then tax deductible (so effectively pre-tax).

The total of these concessional contributions needs to remain below the 'concessional contributions cap' which, as of 2021/22, is $27 500 per annum,[8] an increase from $25 000 per annum (which it has been since 2017/18).

Non-concessional contributions

Additional non-concessional (after-tax) contributions can be made up in the main from:

- **Voluntary after-tax contributions:** These may be from your take-home pay, a lump-sum contribution (for example, from an inheritance) or after selling an asset such as your home. (Selling your home after your preservation age is a special case: see the 'downsizer contribution' in the next section.)

- **Spouse contributions:** These are contributions to your super made by your spouse (whether married or de facto) on your behalf.

- **Government co-contribution:** Under certain circumstances, mainly focused on low- and middle-income earners, the government may 'top- up' a voluntary superannuation contribution with a so-called co-contribution. This currently amounts to a maximum of $500.

Non-concessional contributions are also capped; as of 2021/22, they have increased from the previous $100 000 to a maximum of $110 000 per year. A 'bring forward' rule (with limits) allows you to contribute up to $330 000 in one year, such as if you sell your house and have extra cash, as long as you don't make further contributions for the following two years.

Limits on your total superannuation balance

While you can build up your super by the various methods described so far in this chapter, everyone is limited to a 'Total Superannuation

---

[8] A carry-forward option exists whereby, in certain circumstances, 'unused' concessional contributions in one year can increase your concessional contributions cap in future years.

Balance' (TSB) of $1.7 million,[9] which comprises all their super assets (including both accumulation and pension accounts, but not including earnings generated by those funds).

This applies to individuals, so a couple can accrue twice as much between them. Another rule is the Transfer Balance Cap of $1.7 million,[10] which applies to how much someone can transfer to the pension (retirement) phase. I discuss the benefits of this later in this chapter.

There is one exception to this. The so-called 'downsizer contribution' allows you to add another $300 000 of funds from the sale of your residential home (for example, if downsizing to something smaller) after your 65th birthday.

This limit also applies to individuals, so is effectively doubled for a couple.

How long can I continue to add to my super?

There is no hard-and-fast line at either your preservation age or at 65 that says you must either stop accumulating super or start withdrawing it. After you reach 65, provided you are still working, you can continue to build up your superannuation savings, including receiving employer contributions. Once you reach 67 though, you will need to meet the requirements of a work test for any non-concessional contributions.

Getting money out of super

After you reach your preservation age, it is possible to start withdrawing your accrued superannuation savings. This is the whole idea of super, after all: that you save until retirement, then use your super to maintain your standard of living beyond that point.

---

[9] These figures are based on the 2021/22 financial year. TSB is limited by non-concessional contributions once it goes over $1.7 million but does not include concessional contributions.
[10] These figures are based on the 2021/22 financial year.

All funds added to your superannuation via the methods I described in the preceding sections go into what is called an 'accumulation account'. There are two ways of moving money out of your accumulation account:

- **You can withdraw all or part of your funds as a lump sum and move them 'outside super' into, say, a bank account.** From there you can invest or spend those funds in any way you like. (You would only do this if you had a clearly defined investment strategy for those funds. Simply withdrawing them and leaving them in the bank would not be a tax-effective approach.)

- **You can move funds from your accumulation account to a 'pension income stream'.** This is a special type of superannuation account that pays you a regular 'tax-free' pension. The amount and regularity of this pension is up to you, within defined limits.

  Currently, the requirement is that up to age 65 (where your preservation age is earlier than this) you can withdraw from 4 per cent[11] of the capital of the pension account each year, in one or more payments over the year. This percentage increases from 65 onwards. If you are in transition to retirement, for instance because you wish to continue working part-time, there is a maximum cap of 10 per cent per annum that you can withdraw.

You cannot add additional funds to a pension account once it has been established. However, it is possible to create multiple pension accounts from multiple withdrawals from your accumulation account. So, as you get older, if you want to take a greater pension, you can transfer more funds from your accumulation account to a second (or third, and so on) pension account. The withdrawal obligations apply independently to each pension account.

---

[11]The federal government halved the minimum pension for the 2021/22 financial year to 2 per cent.

Super: The tax haven everyone can use

Superannuation comes with a number of tax benefits. The great thing about these is that everyone with a superannuation account gets to take advantage of them. These benefits apply both when adding to and withdrawing from super.

Tax on super contributions

Concessional (pre-tax) super contributions are taxed at 15 per cent as they move into your superannuation fund. This rate applies regardless of your income level and effective marginal tax rate. For instance, an individual who earns a taxable salary of $100 000 per annum has a marginal tax rate of 32.5 per cent. However, the $10 000 contribution made to their superannuation by their employer (in addition to their salary) will be taxed at only 15 per cent. The 15 per cent rate applies to all concessional contributions, including salary sacrifice contributions and tax deductible personal after-tax contributions up to the concessional contributions cap. (Refer to the earlier section 'Getting money into super'.)

Some variations to the 15 per cent rate apply to low- and high-income earners.

Non-concessional (after-tax) contributions are not taxed on the way into your superannuation fund, on the basis that you have already paid personal tax on those funds. Nor are they tax deductible. As such, there is no tax advantage to non-concessional contributions at the point they are made. These contributions do, however, have tax benefits on their investment returns, and no tax is payable when the funds are ultimately withdrawn.

Returns or *earnings* on your accumulation superannuation account are taxed at 15 per cent, regardless of your income level and effective marginal tax rate. This contrasts with returns on investments outside super that are taxed at your marginal tax rate. So, to continue with the earlier example, should the person earning $100000 per annum make a non-concessional (after-tax) contribution to their superannuation of $10000, which goes on to earn a 10 per cent ($1000) return, that return will be taxed at 15 per cent. For a similar investment of $10000 made outside super, also earning 10 per cent, the earnings of $1000 would be taxed at 32.5 per cent.

Returns or earnings of a superannuation account that has been moved to pension (retirement) phase (refer to the section 'Getting money out of super') *are not taxed*. This is one of those benefits everyone should know about.

The fact that the funds in your pension account are growing tax free is significant, as you want your funds to last as long as possible in retirement.

Tax on super withdrawals

In general, there is no tax payable on money withdrawn from your superannuation fund—provided you have passed 60.

The relevant tax was paid at the point of contribution and on earnings, so no further tax is payable.

This applies to both lump sum and pension account withdrawals. There are a few examples where some small amount of tax may still apply, such as with some defined benefit schemes, but these are rare.

After your death, any funds remaining in your superannuation accounts can be withdrawn by your dependants, also free of tax (with some small exceptions).

Superannuation myths

Let's have a look at some of the common misunderstandings about superannuation.

Myth 1: I'm in my 50s so it's too late to boost my super now

It's true that many people look at their superannuation balance during their early 50s and think they've left themselves short. Depending on their circumstances and work history, that balance may not be very large.

However, in practice it's never too late to save for your retirement or that next phase of life.

After all, many in their 50s have now moved past the expenses of the previous 20 years, particularly around the mortgage, schooling and other child-raising costs. Super can be a tax-effective way of boosting your savings, and this period should be a time when you can focus on topping up your super to the maximum allowed.

The point to emphasise here is that for most people, your focus at this point should be to convert as many non-super assets into super assets before you retire, due to the tax benefits that superannuation offers.

Myth 2: My 65th birthday is a 'magic' date, after which I stop adding to super and start withdrawing from it

While there are rules around accessing your superannuation before the age of 65, there is no reason that this needs to be the date from which you start drawing down your superannuation savings (or stop building them up). You have control over when you stop contributing and/or start withdrawing your funds. In fact, if you keep working as a salary earner, your employer will continue to pay the Superannuation Guarantee Contribution until at least the age of 75 (after which, continuing to make that contribution is optional).

Myth 3: My investment strategy needs to change after I turn 65

Following on from Myth 2, there is no need to change your investment strategy when you turn 65. As we have learnt, a smart, diversified investment strategy in your 40s and 50s should see you generating some good growth in your portfolio, which should continue well into your 60s, 70s and beyond. Those investments don't suddenly become less valuable just because you've turned 65. On the contrary, as life expectancy increases, the chances are that these funds will need to last longer. As long as you maintain a minimum 7- to 10-year time frame in your investment strategy, the same investment principles continue to apply.

Myth 4: A sharemarket crash on my 65th birthday will ruin my retirement

The value of your superannuation fund will rise and fall over time. While it is no guarantee, over 100 years of history suggests that the rises will outweigh the falls over the longer term. Most importantly, volatility in the sharemarket or any other investment class only has relevance at the point you want to sell. So unless you are planning to cash out your entire superannuation savings on the day after your 65th birthday (which would not be a good idea, regardless of market conditions), what the sharemarket does on your big day is irrelevant in the medium to long term.

Myth 5: My money only needs to last 20 years

For someone retiring now at age 65, current life expectancy in Australia is around 84 for a man and 87 for a woman. On this basis, your superannuation and investments may only need to last 20 years on average.

However, there are over 500 000 Australians aged 85 and over, and that number is increasing.

With better health and lifestyle, Australians are living longer. It would be a good idea, therefore, to take a bit of a longer view and make those funds last a few more years if you can. Far better to plan for a long life in retirement than have your money run out early.

Taking control of your superannuation investment

In Chapter 4 I introduced ways of optimising your investment strategy in order to give yourself the best chance of achieving the financial freedom we spoke of in Chapter 3. It's important to understand that you can apply most or all of your chosen investment strategy to the funds you have tied up in super, just as you can to investments made outside of super. This is possible because, as previously noted, while you cannot, as a rule, withdraw your superannuation savings before your preservation age, you can move them around, both within and between superannuation funds and in and out of different investments.

Choosing your employer's super fund versus a retail or industry fund

When joining a new employer, you can decide which superannuation fund you want to use. This is usually a choice between your employer's fund—normally the default option—or a super fund of your own preference (perhaps one you already have an account with). The employer's fund may be an existing retail or industry fund or, in the case of larger employers, they may have their own fund. In practice, most people still opt to join their employer's fund, as most just find it easier, though this may not be the best option.

Traditionally, employer super funds could take advantage of their size to achieve discounts not available to personal accounts within other funds. They therefore had lower fees, which usually meant better investment performance, and could also offer low-cost insurance. Some employers even paid the cost of insurance.

In recent years, retail and industry funds have generally become more competitive in these areas and there tends to be little difference these days.

The best option is usually to check what your employer fund offers at the time you start a new job. If they provide employer-paid benefits, you should take advantage of these. You may be able to roll over your previous superannuation savings into the new fund to simplify matters, but if you do this, make sure you don't lose any benefits, particularly with your insurance cover.

Changing investments within your existing super fund

We have a lot more control of our super than we used to. Within your superannuation fund you will typically be able to choose to split your funds across a range of investments and managed funds.

You can choose the class of investments (for example, cash, Australian shares, international shares or property) or investment multi-asset strategies such as 'growth' (higher returns over time, but also higher volatility), 'high growth', 'conservative' (low risk but generally lower returns) and 'balanced' (usually the default). I discussed these in more depth in Chapter 4.

In most cases you can change your mix of investments at any time within your superannuation fund online account, which means it is very easy to, say, opt for a longer-term high-growth strategy when you are young and reconsider as you get closer to finishing work, depending on your risk profile and your understanding of how this all works. If you find yourself more comfortable with how these funds work and take a longer-term view, sticking with a high-growth strategy may continue to be the best option.

Talking about investing more conservatively as you get closer to retirement could be more about needing to better understand how investments work.

Selecting self-managed super funds

You don't need to rely on a fund, either. A large number of Australians manage their own superannuation in what's called a 'self-managed super fund' (or SMSF), which effectively means that any of the sorts of investment we have discussed (for example, direct shares, managed funds and direct property) can be made under the banner of superannuation.

Self-managed super funds have become very popular because of the level of control they offer and the idea of escaping the fees charged by the super funds. However, they do have their downsides. In particular, they put a lot of responsibility for navigating the complexity of super back onto you, the fund trustee. And while you may save on fees, you will end up spending money on accounting and tax return administration, which can quickly add up. In my experience, unless you have at least $500 000 to invest in your super fund or a specific property you wish to buy inside super, the benefits of an SMSF are marginal.

Using investment platforms or wrap accounts

Investment platforms and wrap accounts, as described in Chapter 4, are frequently available in a superannuation structure. What this means is that you have access to the same diverse range of investments offered by these platforms, but for your superannuation savings. These are the preferred method of investment for the majority of superannuation funds, due to their ease of administration and user-friendly access. Whether retail, industry, public sector, self-managed or employer funds, most are now versions of a platform/wrap account.

Bringing existing investments under super

Australians have long had a love affair with property, with many preferring to build a property portfolio and to live off the rental income. This is an easy-to-understand approach that makes sense as long as a long-term tenant is viable.

However, you do need to understand that the rent you receive from an investment portfolio is taxable at 'normal' (that is, outside super) rates. One option to avoid this is to sell the property prior to retiring and contribute (within limits) the proceeds into your superannuation fund, from which, once retired, you can withdraw the funds tax free. If you operate your own SMSF, the fund could buy another property. Taking this approach would mean the rental income would be tax free, and you could take advantage of a pension stream.

In-specie transfer is a way of transferring assets such as shares or commercial property into an SMSF, in order to access the tax benefits of super without having to sell down these assets first. However, this is a complex approach that I would not recommend pursuing without seeking advice.

A word on MySuper

MySuper is a government initiative introduced in 2014 and designed to simplify superannuation and reduce fees, particularly for those with little interest in choosing a superannuation fund in the first place, or actively managing their super as they approach retirement. MySuper funds are managed funds like other superannuation funds, run by the major superannuation providers. However, they have particular characteristics, including a balanced/growth portfolio and low fees. MySuper funds are the default fund for those who start work and don't yet have a super fund.

MySuper funds, in general, use a similar investment mix, and for many, that mix changes as you get older. Specifically, the funds re-weight their clients' investments as those clients get closer to retirement, shifting away from shares and towards cash. The idea is to reduce the vulnerability of retirees to a major sharemarket crash on the eve of their retirement.

The concern with MySuper funds is twofold.

First, because they are based on a balanced portfolio from the outset, those with money in these funds are potentially missing out on significant earnings over their working lives. Superannuation is a long-term investment and so a growth or high growth portfolio is almost always a better option. (Chapter 4 talks more about your risk-level options.)

Second, the shift to a conservative, cash-heavy portfolio as you get closer to retirement almost always means lower returns, and this in turn means that people's superannuation funds will run out sooner than if their funds were invested in a growth or even balanced portfolio. While it's true that a more conservative portfolio reduces the risk that your super could be devalued on the day you retire due to a sharemarket crash, in practice you won't be looking to withdraw all of your super balance on that day anyway. There is ample time for you to wait for the market to recover. It would be worse if that conversative investment saw your funds run out prematurely, forcing you onto a government pension. This would put greater stress on both yourself and the social security system.

Why is this important to understand? It could be that some or all of your superannuation is currently invested in a MySuper fund. That's fine if that's your choice, but you should know that you do have a choice, and you could roll over these funds into an alternative high-growth-type managed fund if you choose to do so. Check your superannuation statement or website, or with your employer, to see how this applies to your own situation.

Investment strategies for superannuation

In Chapter 4, I discussed the importance of having an investment strategy. This becomes even more important in the decade or so before your 'preservation age', and again after that point.

Put very simply, the typical investment strategy in the years ahead of Year R will focus on growth, shifting to a greater focus on income beyond that point. The specifics will relate very much to your own situation, and I strongly advise seeking advice on this to create the best 'retirement strategy' for you. You usually only get one chance at this, and who wants to be forced back to work rather than enjoying their well-earned retirement?

Optimising your superannuation before 65

As a general rule, the aim of your investment strategy in the decade prior to Year R will be to build up your superannuation savings as much as possible. For many people, with the mortgage paid off, or close to it, and school fees a thing of the past, the 50s age group presents the first opportunity for some time to make substantial savings. You can make even better use of those savings by focusing them on super.

There are a number of reasons for doing this, including the following:

- Planning ahead can allow you to work around the limits on the annual contributions you can make to your superannuation (currently $137 500 per year,[12] made up of both concessional and non- concessional contributions).

- Making these contributions is not restricted to making cash deposits into a super fund. Using an investment platform, you can bring existing investments (such as shareholdings) inside your superannuation.

- Increasing your superannuation balance allows you to take earlier benefit of the tax advantages on superannuation returns (that is, you will pay an effective rate of 15 per cent tax on returns from investments under super, as opposed to paying tax at your marginal rate).

---

[12] These figures are based on the 2021/22 financial year.

Options for maximising your superannuation balance while you are still working

Maximising your super in the 10 or 15 years before Year R means taking maximum advantage of both your concessional and non-concessional contribution 'allowances':

- Maximise your concessional contributions by, where possible, using salary sacrifice to increase the amount your employer pays into your super fund. If salary sacrifice is not available as an option, you can make personal after-tax contributions and claim them as a tax deduction (provided your total concessional contributions are no more than $27 500 per year[13]).

- Maximise non-concessional contributions by making additional after-tax deposits of savings into your super fund and/or by moving existing investments inside super (as described in the earlier section 'Taking control of your superannuation investment').

The other way to build your super balance in this period is to ensure it is well invested. Depending on your personal circumstances and risk profile, this may mean ensuring your funds are invested in growth-oriented investments as opposed to more conservative investments.

Optimising your superannuation after 65

Once you reach your preservation age, your investment strategy around super may change. This is primarily because you are now able to withdraw some or all of your superannuation savings, and you can move funds from your accumulated savings into one or more pension accounts.

Remember, pension accounts have the significant advantage that investment returns are tax free.

---

[13] These figures are based on the 2021/22 financial year.

Options for superannuation optimisation after you finish paid work

Once you move into the pension phase, your focus may shift towards maximising your investment income while preserving your superannuation balance.

General strategies for doing this include:

- **Use account-based pensions.** These accounts provide tax-free income on both withdrawals and the earnings of the fund. They provide great flexibility, as you can decide how often you want to be paid and when, as well as having the option to withdraw lump sums. Your diversified investment strategy can continue within your pension account. When you are ready to live off your own income or even top up a government pension, account-based pensions are a great strategy for doing so.

- **Have one to two years of pension payments available.** Many people are concerned that if there is a fall in the sharemarket, the value of their superannuation savings will drop. As a result, they may avoid withdrawing from their super fund for fear that this will 'crystalise' their losses before the sharemarket, and their super, has a chance to recover.

  This is an understandable response; however it is possible to avoid this risk and create a buffer for yourself by holding one or two years' worth of pension payments in a cash account. Those funds are effectively insulated from sharemarket volatility. You will have the cash to live off while giving the market time to rebound.

  This approach can also be used if you are relying on property income. There is always the risk that you will lose a tenant, leaving your property vacant for a period of time. Again, having some savings set aside in cash would provide you with money to live off until new tenants can be settled in.

This approach gives you breathing space, removing the need to make rash investment decisions in order to access funds at short notice.

- **Access annuities.** Investment companies like Challenger have specialised in providing annuities for retirees for a long time now, although there are not many other options in this area, unfortunately. *Annuities* are where you can set a certain amount to be paid to you monthly, for example. The amount is based on the lump sum you initially invest with the company, and can be guaranteed for life, based on that lump sum.

  Annuities are preferred by people looking for the security of a monthly income rather than having to draw down on their investment capital. You will usually be giving up some return for that security, but annuities can provide comfort and help you avoid sleepless nights if you will otherwise be constantly worried about where the money is coming from and the ups and downs of the sharemarket.

- **Take advantage of being a couple.** While some understand the restrictions on superannuation investments once you reach $1.7 million,[14] many forget that this sum is doubled for couples, so $3.4 million between you. As it is often the case that one partner accrues less superannuation than the other, with a bit of planning, a more equitable strategy can be organised, allowing the two of you to take full advantage of the joint limit.

- **Estate planning.** Ensure you have your beneficiaries set up correctly within your superannuation fund so that if anything happened to one of you, your partner is going to receive the funds easily and tax efficiently. (See Chapter 7 for more on this.)

---

[14] These figures are based on the 2021/22 financial year for the Total Superannuation Balance (TSB).

New Zealand's retirement system

The New Zealand and Australian retirement systems have many similar characteristics. They both provide a tax-effective way to save money now, while working, so that you will have enough for when you retire. Both also see the need for a solution that minimises the need for a future government pension. As with all ageing populations, there will be less people working to pay for government pensions compared to those who have already retired.

The main difference, though, is that the Australian superannuation system is a compulsory scheme that allows additional voluntary contributions, whereas New Zealand's KiwiSaver is a voluntary scheme with a range of extra incentives and flexibility to encourage participation, as well as to suspend participation if needed.

People in New Zealand also have a range of retirement investment options to choose from, just like Australia, and it's important to get this part right.

So much of what I have written about in this book concerns the importance of *maximising your asset allocation* to ensure your funds are working as hard as possible for you, for as long as possible. We are all living longer, which is great—as long as we can afford it!

In a nutshell, there are three parts to the New Zealand retirement system:

- The government pension

- KiwiSaver (a volunteer savings scheme)

- A growing trend for employer-based private sector pension funds.

For simplicity, I am going to look at the pros and cons of the KiwiSaver retirement scheme. And importantly, because it is voluntary, before you decide whether to join or not I suggest you seek financial advice on this.

How does KiwiSaver work?

While everyone in New Zealand is entitled to a government pension, this is only a relatively small amount of money compared to the average salary, and so for many there could be a gap between their pension income and the lifestyle they may wish to achieve in retirement. To help people fill this gap, the government has provided incentives for people to voluntarily save through KiwiSaver.

While KiwiSaver is a voluntary scheme, when you start with an employer, they automatically enrol you into a KiwiSaver program. However, you do have eight weeks in which you can opt out. A range of providers offer KiwiSaver schemes, which is why it's so important to get advice on this.

Once you have a KiwiSaver provider, you will have a range of investment options with different risk levels (such as conservative, balanced and growth) to choose from (refer to Chapter 4 for more on these different levels of risk).

You can choose how much you wish to contribute to your KiwiSaver, which ranges from 3 to 10 per cent (pre-tax) of your salary. You can also make one-off contributions. As an incentive to encourage you to make contributions, your employer will contribute at least 3 per cent as well, and the government will contribute an amount of around NZ$520 to your scheme each year.

One of the clear benefits of KiwiSaver (compared to Australia's super) is that you can withdraw funds for your first home deposit. This is an excellent benefit because for many people, saving for a deposit is the hardest part of purchasing their first home, as by the time they have saved enough (say, over two or three years), the value of a house has increased too, pushing the purchase further out of reach.

Australia's federal government brought in a similar option here in 2017, although you can only withdraw $15 000 at any one time from the extra savings you make. This does limit your options when you look at house prices in major capital cities in Australia compared to New Zealand.

There is also the argument here in Australia that this release of funds should not be allowed, as these funds should be for your retirement. However, my view is that most people need help now to get into their first home in their 20s and 30s, and they will have time to catch up later in life (such as after their children's school fees have been paid).

Comparing each country's retirement scheme

It would be hard to choose between Australia's super and KiwiSaver as both have their own special benefits. However, for me, I am conscious that until superannuation was made compulsory in Australia in 1992, very few people volunteered to make contributions on their own—perhaps they thought that funding their retirement was a problem for another day. Under a compulsory system, at least we know there will be some money by the time we retire.

I do like that New Zealand allows for a much broader first home buyers incentive, however, and that employees must contribute if they are to receive their employer's contribution. I also like that, once retired, government pensions are not means-tested against the assets and income test; it may seem like a minor point, but all the extra paperwork involved does cause a lot of anxiety for many older Australians.

How can I research KiwiSaver further?

New Zealand has an equivalent to the ASIC Moneysmart website called Sorted (sorted.org.nz), which has information on KiwiSaver as well as all other aspects of financial planning, including how to find a financial adviser in your area.

If you want to ensure you will have enough funds to enjoy your retirement and achieve financial freedom, it makes sense to join KiwiSaver if you're in New Zealand. If you do, here are three important points to consider:

- Review which KiwiSaver plan is right for you.

- Work out what contribution level you can afford, as this can be increased over time.

- Consider your investment options to make sure your money is working hard for you.

Overall, also consider speaking to a financial adviser to get advice on these three considerations, as they can do all this research for you and help you prepare for your retirement, and your future.

Some final words on superannuation

I have three final points to mention about superannuation: living overseas in retirement, divorce and superannuation, and getting the right advice (which I cannot emphasise enough).

Living overseas in retirement

For many, living overseas is what retirement is all about. You have worked hard all your life, built substantial assets—or at least enough for a comfortable retirement—and now you want to travel or live overseas. The countryside of Italy beckons!

As we've seen, there are many rules around superannuation, especially when it comes to the favourable tax treatment of pensions and the interest you earn. You should be aware that this can all change if you choose to live overseas for an extended period of time.

There isn't the space here to go into this in detail, but as one example: if you have your own SMSF, one of the responsibilities of running that fund is that its management must take place in Australia.

If you do move overseas, make sure you keep your super fund up to date as to where you are living. The last thing you want is for your super fund to lose touch and move your savings into 'Lost Super' with the ATO.

Divorce and superannuation

The rules around divorce and superannuation have changed recently, with the aim of being fairer in the splitting of super between members of a couple in the unfortunate instance of divorce. In short, superannuation can be counted as an asset by the Family Court and can be split in line with the court's decisions.

This can be significant, as in most couples there will be one partner who has accrued a larger level of super savings. Where assets are to be split equitably, the lawyers can organise an agreement to balance this situation, with consent provided by the Family Court. If the terms are not agreeable to you, you can seek a court order from the Family Court and they will make the final decision as to what is equitable.

Getting advice

The complexity of achieving optimum results, particularly in light of the myriad possible combinations of investment and super structures, really means that seeking professional financial advice should be a high priority in this phase of your life. Getting the right advice and setting up the right plan at the earliest opportunity is very important.

Your action plan and next steps

☐ Write down what you will do once you reach 'Year R'. Make sure you take into account lifestyle, emotional and financial considerations. What will your next big challenge be?

☐ Review your superannuation — how many funds you have, where they are invested, what fees you are paying and what insurance you have.

☐ Have a retirement gap strategy — what do you need to do to close the gap? You may need to change the investment type (say from balanced to high growth) or make extra contributions pre- or post-tax.

☐ Post-Year R, how will you best draw down from your assets, including superannuation, to fund your lifestyle? (A main aim is to pay as little tax as possible in retirement.)

In Chapter 10, I share a full 12-month action plan incorporating many of these actions. In addition, my website (themoneysandwich.com) has plenty of templates, calculators and general information to help you with this process.

Patrick and Amanda's story — the sea change

Patrick and Amanda were both in their late 50s. He was a builder, while Amanda was a part-time legal secretary who had only recently returned to work after taking time off to raise the children.

They came to see me as their third and last child had just left home. Being empty nesters all of a sudden had made them think about retirement. They planned to keep on working for a few years yet. However, years of physical work had taken their toll on Patrick, who now had a bad back. He was going to have to find something, probably in administration, that would be a bit easier on the body.

Realistically, they didn't think they could afford to retire just yet. Patrick had $250 000 in super and Amanda about $100 000. They didn't think that would be enough.

Their other main asset was their home in Hornsby in the north of Sydney. This was worth around $1 800 000 and they had about $60 000 still left on the mortgage after doing some renovations a few years earlier. They had an emergency nest egg of around $20 000 set aside in a separate account.

Their plan was that the mortgage would be paid off in the next few years, though if Patrick stopped work altogether that was going to be difficult on Amanda's salary alone.

Patrick and Amanda told me they had heard the term 'asset rich but cash poor' and felt this was them. They had a valuable home but little else in the way of investments. Being able to afford retirement seemed a long way off.

One thing they were clear about during our first discussion was what they wanted their retirement to look like.

Their dream was to travel around Australia for a few years as they loved the caravanning lifestyle. They would concentrate mainly on the east coast before eventually finding a place to settle. At this stage, they thought Port Stephens would probably be that place: somewhere with a good community, good fishing for Patrick and big enough that Amanda might be able to return to work for a while with a local solicitor.

With a view to making this happen, we worked out together that they would need around $50 000 a year in income once their debt had been paid off. Of that, $40 000 would cover their living expenses and the other $10 000 could be used for travel, renovations and spoiling the grandkids when they came along.

I asked what Port Stephens' property prices were like and Amanda said that they were around the million mark for the sort of house they would be after. However, the area was becoming increasingly popular and they were concerned that they might be priced out of it by the time they were ready to settle down again, a few years into the future.

After this first chat, Patrick and Amanda returned to see me about a week later, by which time I had put together a strategy for them to consider.

What I suggested to them was a bit different—in a good way—from what they'd thought possible.

If they were willing to sell their home now for around the $1.8 million, and buy a home in Port Stephens for around $1 million, they could potentially retire straight away. With that $800 000 difference in value between their current home and what they wanted to buy, they would be able to pay off their mortgage, top up their existing superannuation with $300 000 into each of their super funds and, with the balance, invest into an investment bond. This bond would provide them with sufficient income to live on while travelling, until they were ready to settle down.

The longer they could leave their superannuation alone and allow it to grow, the better off they would be. Aside from the low-taxed earnings on their funds, once they were over 60, they would be able to draw down a tax-free pension from those funds.

The plan included that they could rent out their Port Stephens property while they were fulfilling their caravanning dream. This would bring in additional income. Rather than being 'asset rich but cash poor', their assets would now be better distributed to support their retirement plans. When they were ready to settle down, they would have a home to live in as well as income from their pensions and from Amanda's salary, should she still choose to go back to work. There would even be enough for them to make a gift of $10 000 to each of their adult children.

The following table summarises the before and after of the changes I was suggesting.

	Now — Hornsby	Future — Port Stephens
Home	$1 800 000	$1 000 000
Debt	–$60 000	$0
Super — Patrick	$250 000	$550 000
Super — Amanda	$100 000	$400 000
Cash	$20 000	$20 000
Investment bond	–	$110 000
Gift to children	–	$30 000
Total	$2 110 000	$2 110 000

Patrick and Amanda were rapt to learn that all this was possible. I could see them visibly relax as the potential of this plan sunk in. Being able to retire sooner rather than later was a huge plus, as was the idea of getting into the Port Stephens real estate market before it became any more expensive.

Eight months later, the couple had done exactly what was suggested. They'd sold their home and bought a property in Port Stephens, which they'd then rented out. Now they were on their way with their caravan while, behind the scenes, their superannuation continued to grow as a strong support for their future.

PART 3
Planning for life

In case the unexpected happens

What's in this chapter

The right insurance will preserve your way of life

Building a safety net

Navigating divorce and its aftermath

Life insurance and its relatives

We all like to think that our lives will follow a smooth path, largely uninterrupted by unwelcome events. Many of us will be lucky enough for that to happen but, for others, things won't go according to plan. Health issues can crop up, relationships can break down, natural disasters can strike, salary earners can lose their jobs and business owners can go through dips in income—or even lose their businesses. Sometimes these things build up over time; other times, they come at us from absolutely nowhere. Sometimes they hurt us individually and sometimes, as with the COVID-19 pandemic, the impact is shared widely.

As a member of the sandwich generation, you may be in the fortunate position of having established a reasonably comfortable lifestyle based around owning, or at least close to owning, your own home and living off a steady income. Increased freedom is in sight with healthy, independent parents, and your children are starting to leave school. One day they might even leave home! Perhaps a smooth transition to retirement is on the horizon.

The goal of this chapter is to guide you towards setting things up so that all of this can be shielded from the unexpected with a bit of planning and the creation of a safety net. The alternative is to put your head in the sand and assume that 'it won't happen to me'. Believe me, I've seen (and experienced myself) enough unfortunate situations to know that it could.

Of course, you may already have a safety net in place. If this is the case, it would be a good idea to review this chapter anyway, and possibly to review your plan against your current circumstances. In my experience, even those who have everything in place have often not performed such a review for a while. Does the plan still fit your needs? As you get closer to Year R—and, as we all are, that bit older—it may be that you can reduce your reliance on insurance and focus instead on growing your assets such as super.

The bottom line here is that should the worst happen, you don't want to make it worse for those left behind by not being prepared.

The big points: Your safety net

What you can do right now, no questions asked

1. Log into your superannuation account online, find the 'Beneficiaries' section and check that you have a nominated beneficiary or beneficiaries listed. If you haven't, follow the instructions on the website to make a non-binding nomination

immediately. Most people nominate their partner as the sole beneficiary.

2. While you're in there, find the 'Insurance' section and check how much life insurance, total and permanent disability (TPD) insurance and income protection (sometimes called 'salary continuance') you currently have under your superannuation. Take stock of what insurances of this type you have outside your super as well, including trauma insurance. You might jump ahead to later in the chapter and take our quick assessment to check whether you are under-insured and need more cover, or over-insured and paying too much.

3. Ensure you have a current Will (reviewed in the last five years) and Enduring Power of Attorney. If not, either take the first step towards organising one (or review your current one) now. Not having a Will or having an out-of-date one could cause significant future problems for your loved ones.

4. Check whether or not you would have three months' income available to you at short notice if you needed it. This is our benchmark for financial preparedness in case of the unexpected happening. Two common ways of doing this are by having money set aside in a savings account for this purpose, or the ability to access a redraw facility against your mortgage.

The right insurance will preserve your way of life

The last thing you or your family need in a bad situation is the added threat of losing the family home or having to pull the kids out of school. The right combination of life insurance cover will provide enough money to ensure that life is able to go on as well as it can under any circumstances.

The types of life insurance that will, together, cover most situations, are:

- life insurance

- total and permanent disability (TPD) insurance

- trauma insurance (critical conditions)

- income protection insurance.

The combination of these insurances that is right for you will depend on your particular circumstances. Something you may not be aware of is that there are often opportunities to reduce the cost of these insurances by incorporating them 'inside' your super fund, so effectively paying for them pre-tax. That said, when paying for insurance inside your super, ensure you are aware of the impact the premiums are having on your account balance.

Seeking the advice of a risk (insurance) specialist can sometimes save you thousands of dollars by ensuring you are not paying for life insurance you don't need, and that what coverage you do have is as tax effective as possible.

Who's the most vulnerable in your home?

Before reviewing or planning your safety net, it's worth taking a moment to think about who is the most vulnerable in your home should the unexpected happen. The safety net needs to be set up to protect that person as a minimum.

For instance, who looks after the finances in your family? It's nearly always one half of a couple, and very often the other half will have little to no idea how things are set up or even how to access the bank account other than through an EFTPOS machine. What if something happened to the person 'in charge' of the finances? How difficult would that make life for the other person?

Along the same lines, who looks after the filing system? Who knows where the Wills and other legal documents are stored? What about your insurance policies, and so on?

Is one of you the primary wage earner, while the other works part-time or does volunteer work? What would happen to the mortgage if that primary wage earner's income stopped coming in? Are any investments in one name or the other? Does one of you have more superannuation accrued than the other?

There's a good chance that the person who manages all of this is you, the person reading this book. If that's the case, as you read through the following section and review your own safety net, it's important to consider how effective that net would be if your partner was left to manage everything.

Building a safety net

A good way to think about your safety net is as a way to minimise the disruption that would be caused by a major upheaval. What can you do to ensure that, at the very least, anyone who is left behind is able to keep the house and maintain a lifestyle at a similar level to what it is now?

The answer is usually a combination of making sure your legal paperwork is in order—Wills, Powers of Attorney, and so on—and making sure your financial arrangements are organised to ensure access to cash to keep things going in the short term, plus access to savings and/or insurance that will make sure the bills can continue to be paid over the longer term.

Legal documents to make life easier

It is not the purpose of this book to provide legal advice—I'm not a solicitor—but there are certain documents everyone should have in place but very often don't. In the case of death or traumatic injury, these documents can substantially reduce stress and anxiety for those left behind. Where they don't exist, life can become far more complicated than it needs to be.

Without going into depth, here's a brief explanation of the documents[15] you need:

- **A current and up-to-date Will.** Your Will provides instructions as to the distribution of your estate (that is, your financial assets) in the event of your death. A Will can also provide other instructions to your survivors, such as how you would like your remains treated. The lack of an up-to-date Will can cause significant delays, costs and, potentially, legal disputes in the distribution of your assets to those who are left behind.

- **An Enduring Power of Attorney.** This provides your partner or anyone else you specify with the ability to act on your behalf in 'legal and financial' matters should you die or lose your capacity to make your own decisions. The 'enduring' nature of this document ensures it is ready whenever it is needed.

- **A Deed of Enduring Guardianship.** This provides your partner or anyone else you specify with the power to make 'medical' decisions on your behalf should you be unable to do so.

- **Testamentary Trusts.** (See the following section on this type of trust.)

These documents not only need to be in place, but they also need to be easy to find. If you have a financial adviser, they should be able to refer you to an appropriate lawyer who can assist you with setting up or updating these documents for you. Otherwise ask a friend or work colleague who has had a good experience. In Chapter 7, we discuss this topic further, including law firms who specialise in this area.

---

[15] These names apply to New South Wales, but similar documents exist in all states, if with slightly different names.

You need to understand that dying without a Will (dying 'intestate'), which is sadly all too common, would require your family to hire a lawyer to assist with the long and complex process of applying for probate and proving that no one other than your next-of-kin has any claim to your estate. Even in straightforward cases, this can take many months and be costly, frustrating and stressful.

On my website (themoneysandwich.com) is a Checklist of Important Documents and Important People that should also be safely and accessibly maintained. The list of important people to contact is nearly as important as the other documents themselves.

How the best of intentions can go wrong

There was a legal case in Queensland some years ago that demonstrated the importance of ensuring that your estate planning is up to date and properly thought through.

A couple, let's call them the Lees, in their 50s, had owned a beachfront apartment on the Gold Coast for 30 years. They had spent many enjoyable summers there with their growing son. After their son married, the Lees realised they wanted him and his wife, and children eventually, to be able to enjoy similar experiences. They signed ownership of the apartment over to him.

Tragically, some time later, but prior to having any children, the young couple were both killed in a car crash. This was obviously terrible for both their families, but it became much more complicated when it came time to settle the estates. While the couple both had Wills, Queensland law at the time dictated that if a couple died at the same time, the older of the two was regarded as dying first: in this case the Lees' son. His assets, including the apartment, were therefore inherited by his wife. But as she had also died, those assets were further passed on to the next-in-line of her beneficiaries. As the couple had no children, those beneficiaries were her own parents. The end result was that the Lees not only

(continued)

lost their son and daughter-in-law, but the apartment they had gifted to their son was now solely owned by their daughter-in-law's parents. They had no recourse over this situation.

Had the Lees sought legal advice on their estate, they would likely have done things differently. Perhaps they would have maintained ownership of the apartment themselves, and structured their own Wills so that on their deaths it would have passed either to their son or into a testamentary trust. This would have ensured that the property stayed in the family, regardless of whether the son died, he was divorced, or his circumstances changed in any other way.

Testamentary trusts and the protection of family assets

A *testamentary trust* (also known as a discretionary testamentary trust, or DTT) is a trust that is created by your Will; that is, it comes into effect when you pass away. Testamentary trusts can provide tax and asset protection benefits to your heirs, as well as cushioning the impact of receiving a significant sum of money all at once. They are sometimes referred to as 'bloodline' trusts, as they are often set up to ensure that assets stay within the family line.

The idea of a testamentary trust is that instead of the assets of your estate passing straight to your heirs, those assets are placed into a trust (or trusts—for example, one for each child). It is then up to the trustee of each trust to distribute those assets at their discretion (hence the name). The key difference here is that the assets are 'owned' by the trust, not the beneficiaries.

It's beyond the scope of this book to delve into this too deeply—it's really something you need to discuss with your financial and legal advisers. However, a key point I want to make here is that testamentary trusts can give your intended beneficiaries options for the management of their inheritance that they may not have if they receive that inheritance directly (as in the preceding example of the Lees).

While there are tax benefits available to the beneficiaries of a testamentary trust, as with any trust, our experience is that the more important consideration is the protection provided by such trusts from future creditors and, potentially, Family Court decisions in the case of a divorce. These trusts can be a little bit expensive to set up (anywhere from $1000 to $5000), but this cost is low compared to the legal costs your dependents might encounter if problems arise later.

The importance of superannuation beneficiaries

Aideen is a 65-year-old who became a client of mine after going through a very difficult time following the death of her husband. Unfortunately, dealing with her loss was made much more challenging by a simple oversight: her husband had not nominated her (or anyone) as the beneficiary of his superannuation account.

Let me explain.

When a person dies before their partner, their superannuation fund trustee has to decide who to transfer their account's funds to (including any insurance payouts—which I'll return to). Without any other instructions, the fund's trustee will usually transfer the money to the deceased person's estate, after which it will be divided up in line with that person's Will. In most cases this should be quite straightforward: as in Aideen's case, her husband's Will provided that all his assets be passed to her.

The problem is that this process can take time. It has to wait for the granting of probate (the legal verification of the Will), then the paying off of any outstanding debts and the possible realising or cashing in of any non-cash assets (depending on the Will) before, finally, assets and/or cash can be transferred to the beneficiaries of the Will. This can all take months, even in straightforward cases, which means that people like Aideen can be left without access to the money they need to live comfortably until probate comes through.

All this inconvenience, and the stress that goes with it, can be very easily avoided by nominating beneficiaries to your superannuation fund—in other words, telling your super fund who you would like them to pay in the event of your death. Nominating a beneficiary or beneficiaries gives the fund trustee the authority to pay the account's balance to those people virtually straight away, after the death certificate has been produced—without having to wait for probate.

Had Aideen's husband nominated her as the sole beneficiary of his super fund, that money would have come to her quickly, significantly easing her way forward.

Nominating beneficiaries to your superannuation account is easy. Visit your super fund's website, where you will be able to either nominate beneficiaries on your online account, or download the appropriate form to complete and return to the fund.

Binding and non-binding beneficiaries

Beneficiary nominations come in two flavours: non-binding and binding. A *non-binding* nomination acts as guidance to a super fund's trustee as to where the funds should be distributed, whereas a *binding* nomination, as its name suggests, does not allow the super fund's trustee any say in the matter. You need to seek your own advice on which is the best option for your situation, but I need to emphasise that either option is better than having no nominated beneficiaries at all.

An advantage of the non-binding nomination is that it is very simple and can often be completed online, whereas a binding nomination requires paper forms signed by witnesses. So, often the non-binding option is the easiest place to start. And, to reiterate, it is much better than nothing.

The 'If I wasn't here?' checklist

How prepared would you and your family be if something serious happened to you or your partner? Here is a checklist of documents and other preparations that you should have in place. Should the worst happen, having these in place will help to greatly reduce, for your family, the stress associated with the situation.

It will probably take just one weekend to get all this done, and it will be one of those 'keep you up at night' moments that you can now tick off.

Legal documents

Having all the legal documents prepared (refer to the earlier section 'Legal documents to make life easier'), up to date and accessible is absolutely essential for minimising the stress on your family in the case of your passing.

All of these documents not only need to be prepared, but physical copies need to be securely filed and digital copies made and filed in a location that will be accessible to those who need them. There should also be an up-to-date backup copy of the documents at a different location (for example, one copy on a home computer, one copy in the cloud).

Financial and insurance documents

Most of us accumulate a large number of documents in our modern lives. These should be scanned and stored (digitally) in a way that can be readily accessed by family members, the executor of your Will and, potentially, legal and professional advisers. The documents we're talking about here include mortgage or house title, financial and tax records and insurance policies.

Details of financial circumstances

Records of and access to your day-to-day financial matters will also be important to anyone to whom you have granted Power of Attorney. These include any bank accounts, credit cards, and so on, along with any regular payments (for example, charitable donations and subscriptions).

Online account logins

Your family and/or attorney will likely need to be able to access online accounts to close or pause them. For instance, what do you want to happen to any social media accounts?

Details of important people

The contact details and reasons to call each of the important people in your life—family, friends, employers, professional advisers, medical professionals, and so on—should be readily available. These days it is usually possible to make this sort of critical information available on your smartphone via an emergency access feature.

This list is often overlooked as, of course, you know who your contacts are. But does your partner, your adult children and your executors? We often find that some of these contacts are different for both members of a couple, so it's important that you compile this list together.

Online programs to help

There are some great online services available that can help with secure offsite storage of these documents. We use and recommend a product called Now Sorted for our clients. (For the purposes of full disclosure, the founder, Eddie Lees, was my first boss and mentor. He became passionate about document security after a health scare of his own and finding the need to get his estate documentation organised.) With their permission, I have provided some of their information on our website for your reference, or you can head to the Now Sorted website (nowsorted.com) and click on Resources for useful downloads.

Financial backup to smooth the path forward

When one of the main income earners in a household is incapacitated or worse, it can obviously have an enormous and rapid effect on the rest of the household's ability to pay the bills. In the short term, this only adds to the enormous pressure of the situation. In the longer term, it can threaten the family's standard of living, including, potentially, their ability to keep the roof over their heads. Creating a financial safety net therefore requires that you consider how the income 'hole' can be plugged in both the short and longer terms.

Short-term cash

No matter how bad things get, the world keeps moving and the bills keep coming. A good way to avoid adding to the enormous stress of an unexpected event is to ensure that there is cash that can be readily accessed. There are numerous ways to do this, but two of the most common ways are:

- **Having around three months of salary stashed away in a separate but accessible savings account.** This might take a little while to accrue, but it is the simplest option if you can manage it. After thousands of Australians found themselves out of work due to the COVID-19 pandemic, it was revealed that many did not have even one month's savings available to fall back on. This was one reason why the government temporarily allowed people to dip into their superannuation savings.

- **Having an offset or redraw facility attached to your mortgage so that the equity in your home can be easily and instantly accessed via internet banking.** At the same time, make sure that this doesn't become a source of 'easy' money that unnecessarily puts you into more debt by being drawn on prematurely —Chapter 2 covers debt in more detail.

Longer-term income

In order for anyone left behind after an unwelcome event to be able to maintain their lifestyle, they will need a steady source of income to replace the income lost. This can come from various sources, including:

- ongoing income from existing investment returns, such as a rental property or shares, though these may not be sufficient to replace a lost income

- access to a partner's superannuation savings

- ongoing or lump-sum payments from life insurance or other insurance policies.

Where money is received as a lump sum from either superannuation or insurance, obviously strategies will need to be put into place to make the best use of that money.

Navigating divorce and its aftermath

Divorce can happen suddenly, especially if you are the one left behind. Obviously, there will be nervousness and anxiety about the future, but these emotions can be exacerbated if you find yourself completely unprepared for life on your own. If you have never looked after the finances before in your marriage, having to do all this yourself can be particularly daunting.

Even if the divorce leaves you with enough assets or funds to continue your life comfortably, not knowing where to turn or what to do to keep control of your finances means you can feel very alone and out of your depth. This is even worse if the divorce reduces your income and increases your financial obligations, potentially forcing you back to work at or around the time you would otherwise have been thinking about retirement. Year R will seem a long way off.

If you find yourself in this situation, the best thing to do—in line with my message from the very start of this book—is to start with the basics. Now's the time to build an understanding of money and slowly take control of your finances. I understand that this can be tough, but like learning another language it is essentially just another skill that can be learnt and mastered with practice and the right advice. Even if you would prefer to outsource much of your financial planning and management to others, it is still important to have a good understanding of the basics, so that you can now be in control of conversations you have with your accountant and financial adviser.

Prior to divorce

After separation but before formal divorce, you will need to build a full understanding of your financial position for your divorce lawyer. You also need this to gain clarity of what you'll need in the way of ongoing income into the future, including enough to cover your accommodation (or the mortgage on your home), day-to-day expenses and child-related or young-adult support expenses (where relevant).

There will clearly be a lot to do that is not related to the financial aspects of your life, though I'm going to keep the focus on the financial issues here.

The time to start learning some of the basics of money management is as soon as possible. Debt management, property ownership and superannuation, for instance. You'll likely need to set up bank accounts in your name. (It's not uncommon for joint bank accounts to be frozen while divorce proceedings play out.)

Start creating a list of things to do, research useful websites, and speak to advisers or other people who could help you through all this. There is no need to do this on your own. Tapping into professionals who can provide objectivity but be there for you is very important. The more prepared you are about what you need out of a divorce settlement financially, the easier it will be for your lawyer.

After the divorce

Regardless of the financial situation you are left with after the divorce has been settled, you will need to now make some major financial decisions. Try not to rush into anything. It may feel like you need to do everything at once, but most things can be given some time to get right. The following is not a complete list, but it includes some points to consider:

- **Accommodation.** Should you rent or buy? This decision may be easy if you've stayed in the family home, but if the home was sold in the settlement, you may feel you need to buy something quickly to replace it. However, unless you know the market well, you don't want to rush into this decision. Choosing to rent for a short period of time until things settle down is just fine.

- **Savings.** By now you will likely have set up new bank accounts, but now is the time to start building a three-month nest egg for emergencies, or setting up a redraw facility on your mortgage. (Refer to the earlier section 'Short-term cash' for more.)

- **Budget.** You may not have had to worry about this before and possibly you may not need to in the future, but at the beginning it is worthwhile ensuring you are in control of your cash flow. (Chapter 1 may be helpful here.)

- **Update important documents.** Post-divorce, you will probably want to rearrange the documents relating to you and your estate. You'll likely need to have a new Will and Enduring Power of Attorney drawn up, and the beneficiaries on your superannuation and insurance policies will need to be updated.

Over time, things will likely settle down. Eventually, you will probably start to feel more confident with your money and can start looking to the future. Other areas, like buying property, reviewing your superannuation investment strategy and other investment options, are all matters you can now start to pursue or get advice on. And remember: it's never too late, even if you feel like you are starting from scratch all over again.

Life insurance and its relatives

When I raise the topic of life insurance with a new client, the reaction is predictable: a sceptical look in the eyes as if I'm about to sell them day-old bread. Many remember the now-old-fashioned experience of life insurance being sold as 'whole of life' policies via cold calls over the phone or from door-to-door salespeople.

On top of that, life insurance is not as exciting to discuss as money or shares. Nevertheless, it is an important topic to cover and get right.

Life insurance has changed. Today, the various forms of life insurance policies can be a low-cost addition to your safety net, ensuring that you and your family would be able to stay afloat financially after a dire unexpected event. As such, life insurance can fill any gap between that desired lifestyle and the other forms of financial backup we've discussed so far in this book.

Unlike the movies or crime novels, life insurance is not about the family getting rich from your demise (or that of your partner). It's about allowing those left behind to live with dignity and comfort.

Types of 'safety net' life insurance

The four main types of life insurance relevant to your safety net are term insurance (often also called life insurance), TPD (total and permanent disability) insurance, trauma insurance and income protection. All of these should be carefully considered for you and your partner because they effectively require you to think about the value of your lives, which is obviously a different matter than knowing the value of your cars or home.

Insuring your life is not the same as insuring the car or house

There's an important distinction to be made between life insurances and so-called 'general' insurance policies.

General insurance is the routine insurance you take out to cover your car, your house and contents, your travel, and so on. Health insurance falls into this category as well. General insurance is relatively straightforward to understand because it's insurance that covers things that have a more-or-less easily defined value: the cost of replacing your car, your house or paying hospital bills.

Life insurance, on the other hand, provides ongoing financial coverage in the case of disability or death, which means you have to decide, to put it crudely, what your life is worth and therefore

(continued)

how much cover you need. You should be able to answer the question, 'If the worst happens and I die prematurely, how can I ensure that my family have the ongoing financial resources they need to sustain their lifestyle and their plans for the future?' That's clearly a very different matter to the cost of repairing your house after a storm.

Term (life) insurance

Term insurance policies, often also referred to as *life insurance policies*, are normally structured in a way that they pay the policy holder a lump sum in the event of the death of the life insured. (The person insured can be, and often is, also the policy holder.) The premium will depend on how much cover you have (that is, the size of any potential payout), your age and any health issues. Some health issues can result in higher premiums ('loadings') or even exclusions if they are pre-existing conditions.

Many people we talk to believe they have sufficient life insurance because they know they have some through their superannuation. However, they rarely know how much cover that insurance is providing. Life insurance is indeed provided (at a cost) on an opt-out[16] basis by most superannuation funds, but the level of cover provided is frequently lower than needed to provide a sufficient safety net.

Now is as good a time as any to review what life insurance cover you have, both inside and outside your superannuation.

How much life insurance do I need?

The level of life insurance cover you take out is very much a function of your personal circumstances. It also needs to be considered alongside the other resources in your safety net, including cash savings, superannuation and other investments.

---

[16] For those under 25 years old or with a balance of less than $6000 in their account, superannuation funds are obliged to offer insurance only on an opt-in basis. See more about this in Chapter 8.

For most people, there are four major factors to consider:

- If you have a mortgage, any life insurance payout should pay that off at a minimum. It would guarantee the roof over the family's head and remove the stress of ongoing mortgage payments. If you have any other significant debts or guarantees, consider including enough cover to clear those as well.

- Particularly for the sole or major income earner in the household, how much money would be needed to cover that person's salary or other income until the kids finish school, or possibly later? In the case of a stay-at-home parent, how much would it cost to replace them with a nanny and housekeeper?

- If you are currently paying school fees, you probably want to ensure that those fees are covered by your life insurance and/or other financial safety net. Similar consideration could be applied to the costs of tertiary education, such as university fees, along with any other ongoing costs associated with your children (for example, for a child with a disability).

- If you are assisting, or may need to assist in the future, parents with the cost of aged care, you need to include that cost in the equation as well.

The overriding question here is how much money would be needed to cover and maintain your family's lifestyle at the level they are used to, considering current and future factors?

The following table provides a typical family example:

Term (life) insurance needs — quick guide

Name	Rob	Veronica
Mortgage discharge	$500 000	$500 000
Replace income ($70K pa)*	$700 000	$200 000**
Education funding (6 × $20K)	$120 000	$120 000
Anything else	$0	$0
Life insurance needs	**$1 320 000**	**$820 000**

* As a rule of thumb, to replace salary until retirement, multiply by 10; to replace for lifetime, multiply by 20.

** For the cost of a nanny part-time for 10 years, depending on age of children.

Note that in this situation the assumption is that Veronica would only need to replace her husband's income until her retirement in 15 years, using the '10 times' rule of thumb. With compounding interest, the 10 times rule can make funds last at least 15 years, or up to 20 years. After that, with her children likely leaving home and her ability to access both her husband's super (paid on his death) and her own, she would have enough income to support herself through retirement.

This assumes that she and her husband will have enough superannuation savings accrued, which is often not the case. In situations where a couple is likely not to have sufficient super by Year R, it is better to include 20 times the annual salary, rather than 10 times, in the term insurance calculation. Of course, the numbers in this table are only an example, and they do not account for other factors such as existing asset holdings and future investment returns.

Try this for your own situation with the Your Life Insurance Calculator at themoneysandwich.com to see if you are under- or over-insured.

The mechanics of life insurance payouts

These days, most people have some or all of their term insurance sitting inside their superannuation. Where that is the case, in the circumstance of a premature death, the life insurance payout is simply added to the superannuation balance before it is paid—after the fund receives a death certificate—to the fund's beneficiaries or to the estate (refer to the earlier section 'The importance of superannuation beneficiaries').

For term insurance held outside superannuation, a similar situation applies, except that the insurance company will need to be dealt with separately from the superannuation company. As with superannuation, it is very important that the intended beneficiaries of the term insurance have been named on the policy.

Unlike superannuation, you can have a wider range of people or entities nominated as the beneficiaries of your term insurance. These may include a key person in a business, or adult children who are no longer dependent but who you would want to help out financially. Having nominated beneficiaries will greatly speed up processing and allow the payment to be made to them directly, rather than via the more time-consuming route of the estate. On the other hand, there are some circumstances in which it is preferable to have the estate as the beneficiary. This is beyond the scope of this book and I would strongly advise that you seek advice relevant to your own situation.

Be careful about who owns the policy

In most cases, the life insured on a term insurance policy is also the owner of that policy. However, there are cases where an individual owns a policy on someone else's life. A common example is in the case of a business partnership, though it can also occur in marriages. These can be tricky situations, as whoever owns the policy has final say over the distribution of any payout. For example, we have seen cases where a business has closed or a marriage has finished acrimoniously, but life insurance the partner or spouse had on each other was left in place.

As long as the policy owner keeps paying the premiums, the person whose life is insured cannot cancel the policy, even if they want to. This can result in the strange situation that an ex-business partner would benefit if anything happened to you while your family may not. With this in mind, it's important that for any policy on your life, whether you own it or not, you establish a legal agreement at the outset that gives you some control of this insurance if, say, the business closes.

TPD and trauma insurance

There are, of course, potential situations in which you permanently lose the ability to earn your income and incur ongoing medical costs due to a serious accident. It's for these situations that total and permanent disability insurance (TPD) and trauma insurance exist. These insurances are similar but have some important differences. They are often complementary.

TPD insurance

TPD cover provides a lump sum payment if you become totally and permanently disabled due to an illness or injury. Twenty or 30 years ago this was the standard form of 'personal disaster' insurance on the market. However, in more recent years, due to advances in medicine, it has become harder and harder to prove that the impact of an injury or illness is permanent. For instance, some cancers are not the death sentence they once were, with many people returning to life as 'normal' after a (sometimes extended) period of convalescence.

These factors, along with the rising cost of TPD cover, have led to it not being as popular as it once was. TPD cover usually goes hand in hand with life cover under superannuation so, as with life insurance, you should make sure you are aware of your level of cover and how much you are spending on it. Like life insurance, TPD insurance premiums rise as you get older.

Calculating how much TPD cover you need is similar to considering the four factors outlined for life insurance in the earlier section 'How much life insurance do I need?' After all, if you are permanently disabled, clearing debt and providing an alternate income stream for you and the family are just as important. Most insurance under super funds includes life cover and TPD cover at the same levels for this reason.

Trauma insurance

Trauma insurance, which is also called critical conditions or critical illness cover, provides a lump sum payment under a wider range of conditions than TPD insurance. It will provide a payment should you contract a serious medical condition, even if that condition is not permanent. Heart conditions, stroke and cancer fall into this category. At the very least, trauma insurance can fill the gap between stopping work and when your income protection kicks in.

Due to the diversity of potential situations, and associated medical costs, in which you can make a claim on trauma insurance, it can be difficult to work out how much cover will be enough. An unexpected but reversible heart condition obviously has less significant implications than, say, a diagnosis of multiple sclerosis.

As a rule of thumb, for a couple, I would suggest considering cover for each of you equivalent to at least one to two years' salary of the highest wage earner plus, if you can afford it, enough to pay off any outstanding debts. Consider also your current level of health insurance when making this decision and, of course, your personal circumstances.

TPD and trauma cover are often overlooked, probably because of a philosophy of 'it won't happen to me'. Unfortunately, experience demonstrates that when a major illness or accident strikes—and it can happen to anyone—stress about the financial impact can really hamper the victim's recovery. These insurances don't need to be expensive (depending on how much cover you choose), but they can provide significant peace of mind so are worth considering.

Are you worth the risk?

Current statistics[17] suggest that around 70 per cent of us will suffer with cancer, a heart condition, a stroke or another major trauma in our lifetimes. Yet, less than 20 per cent of people take out trauma cover. At the same time, virtually everyone insures against their house burning down or their car being stolen, despite the risk of either of these being far lower than 70 per cent. It makes you wonder how it is that we seem to place more value on our home or car than on our own lives or those of our loved ones.

Trauma cover is just as important for both of you

Mike had been the main breadwinner in his family since he and his wife Amanda had made the decision that she would stay home while their children were school age. While the kids were at school and money was a bit short, they had decided to concentrate on ensuring Mike was well covered with income protection, life insurance and some trauma insurance. It made sense to cover the main breadwinner, as if anything happened to Mike, his salary would stop. How would they pay the mortgage and meet their day-to-day living expenses? Amanda had a small amount of life insurance through her super fund, but no trauma cover. The couple maintained private health insurance as well.

After the kids had finished school, the couple reviewed their life insurances. As Mike was now in his 50s, the premiums on his insurances had become quite expensive. Also, with a higher level of savings behind them and good superannuation balances, they felt comfortable reducing Mike's level of income protection cover. With some of the money they saved, they took out trauma insurance of $100 000 for Amanda.

---

[17] Australian Burden of Disease Study (2011) and Australian Cancer Research Foundation (2018).

Unfortunately, Amanda developed breast cancer in her early 50s. It was picked up early and after surgery she was given a positive prognosis for the future. All of a sudden, the investment in Amanda's trauma insurance was well worthwhile. While their private health cover definitely helped, the trauma insurance payout allowed Mike to take some extended leave from work to care for his wife.

Speaking to Amanda six months later, she told me the trauma insurance payout had been a godsend. The funds had arrived only five days after they made their claim, greatly reducing the stress of the situation. Then, having Mike at home had helped her recover far more quickly — especially as she had no concerns about his salary not coming in over that period.

With some extra cash left over from the insurance payout at the four-month mark, Mike and Amanda were able to get out of the city for a week up the coast, away from hospitals and doctors' waiting rooms. The relaxing break was a nice bonus.

Amanda saw her trauma payout as a large part of her having a stress-free recovery, free of worry about how the bills would be paid.

She was able to simply concentrate on staying positive and getting better.

The lesson for Mike and Amanda was that it's not just the breadwinner who needs insurance cover.

Income protection insurance

Income protection insurance is fairly self-explanatory. It provides a replacement for up to 75 per cent of your income should you lose the ability to earn that income through illness or injury, either for the medium term or permanently. If this cover is under superannuation, it is also known as Salary Continuance Cover.

Of all the types of insurance we are discussing in this section, income protection is the only one that provides ongoing, regular payments as opposed to a single lump sum.

I see income protection cover as perhaps the most important of the 'safety net' life insurances.

While life cover protects others such as your family in the event of your death, income protection insures your lifestyle under many other (and frankly much more likely) circumstances. It's your income that determines the way you live, how much you travel and other plans for the future. If your income suddenly stopped, it would cause major upheaval for you and your family, so it is worth protecting.

This is even more relevant if you are self-employed as your business is dependent on you being able to work to provide the cash flow, and this all stops if you are off work for any length of time. For some self-employed people, income or revenue can fluctuate significantly, so it's important to ensure the policy contract you have will meet your needs as a business owner if you ever need to claim and provide proof of your income.

The main factors that affect income protection premiums are:

- **the monthly amount you will receive in the event of a claim.** While this will depend on what your actual income is at the time of the claim, you can decide the level, based on up to 75 per cent of your current income (which you will need to demonstrate).

- **the length of the waiting period between the claim and when the payments start (usually 30, 60 or 90 days).** You can decide this too, based on your comfort level and the cost of the premium.

- **the maximum length of time that payments will continue to be made after the first one.** For example, it may be five years, 10 years or until you reach 65.

- **your age and health situation, as with all these safety net insurances.**

Income protection insurance is surprisingly underused in Australia, with only around 33 per cent of people taking it up. It is another great example of the 'it won't happen to me' mindset. Yet it is the most likely of the safety net insurances that people would need to claim if they were prevented from working due to a common health condition or a serious accident (such as a car accident, a bike crash or falling from a ladder).

Unlike the other safety net insurances, income protection (if taken up outside super) is tax deductible, making it an even more attractive proposition.

Life insurance: should it be inside or outside your super?

Of the insurances discussed in this section, life insurance, TPD and income protection (but not trauma insurance) are all commonly available as an 'add on' to your superannuation. That is, the premiums are paid from your superannuation savings. This can have tax benefits because it means the premiums are effectively coming out of savings accrued from pre-tax contributions to your super, rather than from your after-tax income.

Depending on your income level, this can equate to a significant saving on how much you are paying for this insurance.

(Income protection is tax deductible, but obviously if you gain the tax advantage at the point of paying the premium, you are not waiting until you complete your year-end tax return to get that tax back.)

On the flip side, making payments from your superannuation savings obviously reduces your super balance, and so your future super earnings. This needs to be a consideration when reviewing your level of life insurance cover.

Let's say the current life insurance policy inside your super provides $100 000 of coverage, and you wish, on review, to increase that to $1 million. That would likely lead to a 10-times increase in your life insurance premium—from $100 a month to $1000, say. Over 10 or

(continued)

20 years or more, that is going to represent a significant bite into your superannuation balance and its earnings. The best strategy in this instance would usually be to make sure you top up your super for the difference via additional contributions, either through salary sacrifice (if available) or after-tax contributions. Both of these options are going to be better than paying the premium directly from after-tax income.

As a general rule, insurance taken out under your superannuation is going to provide better value than similar insurances taken out outside your super, due to the effective 15 per cent tax discount provided by superannuation. Just be mindful of the impact of the premiums on your super balance, and consider topping up your super with extra contributions.

Adjusting your level of cover as you age

Insurance premiums for all these life insurances tend to increase as you get older, simply because the statistics show that the likelihood of a claim increases with age, and most insurance is provided on the basis of *stepped premiums*, meaning the premium increases each year while the payout remains constant.

On the other hand, hopefully your financial circumstances have also become more stable and secure as you get older. Your children (fingers crossed!) start to make their own way and become less financially dependent on you, while the value of assets such as your home and your superannuation savings should increase. As a result, you can look to your assets as forming a greater proportion of your safety net and reduce your level of insurance cover accordingly, eventually possibly even cancelling it after consideration.

Should the premiums be stepped or levelled?

In most cases, life insurance policies default to become 'stepped' premiums, meaning the premium increases each year while the payout remains constant. The rationale here is that as you age, the risk of the policy being paid out (that is, of you dying or becoming disabled) increases. This is usually not a significant factor when you are young, but the premiums can get very expensive once you are in your 50s.

An option is to ask for a quote for *level premiums* when you are younger, which will be higher initially, but then usually remain unchanged unless you adjust them yourself. For our clients, we recommend this as a no-brainer for all their adult kids, especially for trauma cover (refer to the section 'Trauma insurance', earlier in this chapter), even if they have to pay for it initially until their children have left home. Those premiums will be higher initially, but then usually remain unchanged unless you adjust them yourself. This can end up saving you thousands over the life of the policy, while also make retaining the policy much cheaper later in life, when many around you are cancelling or reducing their cover because of the high cost.

Should you have all four insurance types?

This is not an easy question to answer as your needs will vary with age. When you are young, you would not need all four types of insurance (term, or life; TPD; trauma; and income protection). If you are not married and don't have much debt, consider only trauma cover and income protection. The same may apply when you are close to retirement and have paid off your home and built up assets such as your superannuation. These assets then become your 'safety net', rather than insurance.

In your middle years, when you are most in debt, married with children, all four insurances are likely necessary and they should be part of any comprehensive financial plan. A medium-term illness such as cancer could keep you off work for a year or more, so having trauma cover for an initial lump sum and then income protection until you return to work would be important. If you suffered a long-term, permanent disability, you would need TPD cover to provide a lump sum to help cover rehabilitation and

(*continued*)

lifestyle changes, as well as income protection to pay an alternate salary until you reach 65. Lastly, if you were to pass away, you would need term insurance to ensure your family were well looked after and any debts paid off.

As no one knows what the future holds, there will be a major period of your life when all four covers would be prudent. It then comes down to what your budget can afford. The Your Life Insurance Calculator on themoneysandwich.com may be helpful, or seek out an insurance specialist for advice.

The benefits of a financial (life insurance) adviser

All licensed financial advisers can provide life insurance advice, just like they can for superannuation or shares. However, some do specialise in life insurance as it is a complex and technical area of advice.

You can go direct for life insurance policies but that involves doing your own research. Unless it is something you enjoy doing, a specialist who deals with this every day will most likely be able to find more appropriate policies and will usually save you money.

Another reason to use a specialist is to assess how much cover you need. As I have often heard from clients, 'We're okay as we have insurance already.' Once you go a bit deeper and ask what type or how much, it was likely only $50 000 to $100 000 term (life) cover under their super fund. This would not clear the average mortgage, let alone provide enough for the family they may leave behind.

Finally, when it comes to making a claim, having someone who can act on your behalf (and for your family), rather than dealing with it all by yourself, is incredibly important. Most claims go straight through, but forms still need to be completed or medical information provided. If there are any grey areas, having someone who knows how to speak the insurer's language can be invaluable.

Claiming on an insurance policy

Making a claim on any of these insurances can feel very daunting. However, life insurance companies have, to their credit, spent a lot of time improving their systems and service to ensure as smooth a process as possible.

They usually have a direct line, so you don't have to spend hours waiting on a 1800 number to get through. Once notified, they will send you a claims kit that shows, step by step, the process to follow and what is needed to complete the claim. If you have an adviser, contact them first and they will organise this for you as part of their service. Most claims are sorted out and paid very quickly and efficiently, though there are always cases where there are issues or difficulties. Having an adviser to liaise on your behalf does help.

If you have a complaint or your claim has been denied for whatever reason, there are, importantly, steps in place to help you. You always have recourse. All life insurers have to provide you (usually with the claim kit) with instructions on how to make a complaint to their internal dispute resolution (IDR) department. Strict timelines apply to when they need to respond to you. If this does not resolve your complaint, then you can apply to AFCA (Australian Financial Complaints Authority), the industry watchdog, to have them hear your complaint. If, after all this, you are still not satisfied, you can apply to take the insurer to court as a last resort.

When should you seek legal advice for a claim?

As with any type of complaint, the steps that have been put in place to protect you are all available without cost and, especially with AFCA, are totally independent. Approaching a law firm will cost money in fees or a percentage of your claim, so I would only recommend doing so if all else fails. Research confirms that most claims are paid and, for the few that aren't, many get settled through the insurer's internal dispute department or AFCA.

(continued)

> While lawyers do play an important role if these normal resolution procedures don't work, I see them as a last resort, rather than a first step, as some advertising suggests.

Types of 'safety net' general insurance

What is not covered under life insurance is often referred to as *general insurance*, which can include health insurance (although it is often a category all on its own). General insurance includes the main areas such as house, car and business, but also includes areas such as travel, pet and marine insurance, to name a few.

As with life insurance, general insurance should be part of any good financial plan as a safety net to protect you and your family's assets and future.

Car insurance

It is compulsory to have insurance for your car but as there are a range of car insurances, you may not be fully aware of the different types and why you may need them. Some also may not realise that while they have car insurance under their own registration, it may be very limiting if it does not cover themselves or their car, and only covers the other person in a car accident.

There are three main types of car insurance:

1. **Compulsory third party insurance (CTP) or 'Green Slip'.** This is the basic cover required by law and is part of your car's registration cost. This cover provides monetary protection if you injure or kill someone in a car accident, but it does not cover you, your passengers or either car.

2. **Extra insurance, such as third party property, fire and theft insurance.** This provides monetary protection if you damage the

other person's car or property in a car accident. You can also add on fire and theft if, for example, you leave your car parked on the street regularly.

3. **Comprehensive car insurance.** If you can afford this (as it is the most expensive), it is recommended as while it also includes cover for the other car or property in an accident, it importantly covers your car for all repairs and damage, even if the accident is your fault. This also covers your car if it is stolen, or damaged by flood or fire, although contracts differ so be sure to check the wording.

As insurance can become expensive, most policies offer an *excess*; that is, you can pay an initial amount, if you make a claim, that lowers the regular premiums. One other important point to understand is whether you are insuring your car at *market rate*, as this will go down over time as the car decreases in value, or at an *agreed value rate*, which keeps the car's initial value but requires a more expensive premium.

Comparison websites can help you review the different types of cover and premiums available, so be sure to do some research so you understand exactly what you're paying for.

Home insurance

Just like car insurance, home insurance should be part of any good financial plan as you never know when mother nature will decide to do her worst. While you hope you never have to use it, insurance does provide that comfort factor in case the worst does happen.

There are two types of home insurance:

1. **Building insurance:** As the name suggests, this insurance covers you financially for repairing or replacing your home should something happen. You may have a set price or sum that you insure for although, over time, it may end not being enough and so a *total replacement sum* insured is another option, although more expensive.

2. **Contents insurance:** This insurance provides cover for all your household items and personal belongings in the house. If you were renting, this would typically be all you would need. It's important to itemise your contents, especially costly items such as jewellery.

You can insure your home with these two types of insurance separately or as a combined package (which is the most common option). Depending on the type of policy, it may also cover storms and flooding, for example, but you need to check as some have optional extras that may need to be paid for on top of your regular premium.

It's worth doing the research to find the best policy for your home, and comparison websites are available to help you decide on the best option. Also, remember to review your policy every few years to ensure you are getting the best value for money.

Business insurance

If you are self-employed or even running a sizeable corporation, there will always be risks worth covering in case the worst happens. Areas such as theft through to personal and public liability (such as if a customer slipped over on the premises), right up to the more recent phenomena of cyber-attacks, all need to be considered when you're running a business. Also, business insurance can protect you, your employees and your business in case you or an employee have an accident while at work.

Anyone in business should seek advice on what is appropriate to their situation. This way you can get the advice you need on the most appropriate business insurance policies, tailored to your business or situation. I have always found that using a specialist business insurance broker saves me time and money. I also like that insurance brokers represent you, not the insurer. Every business is different, so rather than trying to do it all yourself, you can get on with what you're good at—running your business.

Finally, if you ever need to make a claim, if you use a broker you will appreciate the benefits of having someone act on your behalf rather than you having to deal with it all by yourself.

Insurance myths

Let's have a look at some of the common misunderstandings about insurance.

Myth 1: Insurance companies don't pay claims

It is interesting how many people use the idea that insurance companies don't pay up as a reason to not take out cover. Nothing could be further from the truth. In terms of life insurance (which is the only one I have direct experience of in this regard), insurance companies pay billions every year in claims and, according to the Australian Securities and Investments Commission (ASIC) and the Australian Prudential Regulation Authority (APRA), the regulators of the life insurance industry, over 90 per cent of all claims are paid.

Retail policies (that is, individual policies) are associated with a higher payout percentage than group policies under super. This makes sense, as with retail policies you have an adviser who assists with any claim. In addition, retail policies have more stringent underwriting than policies under group super; however, the differences are small.

Myth 2: I would be better to invest my money than spend it on insurance

It's true that if you never make a claim, money spent on insurance is money that you won't get back. However, life is unpredictable, and we just don't know what the future will bring. We take out insurance on our cars hoping we will never have to claim, and really the same logic applies to life insurances. These provide a 'safety net' to protect you and your family for only a few cents on the dollar (to what you would receive), so it just makes sense for peace of mind. Locking in 'level premium' rates when young (refer to the earlier section 'Adjusting your level of cover as you age'), when you have few assets and low debt, can keep your premiums locked at that time and give you the opportunity of maintaining those lower premiums into the future.

Myth 3: Only the breadwinner needs to be covered

Where there is a main breadwinner in the family, it is particularly important to have that person covered by life insurances. However, a stay-at-home or lower-income partner should also be covered, especially if you are raising children at that time. If anything happened to that person, the cost of a nanny and/or housekeeper would be substantial, and the breadwinner may need to take time off or reduce their hours to care for the children.

Myth 4: All insurers are the same

Just like any product, insurance policies have changed and evolved over time. Thirty years ago, insurance didn't differentiate between smokers and non-smokers when it came to life insurance premiums or health insurance. Twenty years ago, trauma insurance only covered three conditions, where now it provides cover for over 30 conditions. It's worth choosing policies that meet your particular needs, or perceived needs.

Like their products, insurance companies themselves are worth comparing, as there have been major changes over the last five years. Some companies that have been around for 100 years or more have now merged or been sold off, while traditional companies like Zurich, AIA, MLC and TAL are still here (and continue to evolve themselves, offering health and wellbeing programs, for example), and new retail providers like Integrity and MetLife are providing added competition.

Like your superannuation or any other investment, reviewing your cover on a regular basis to ensure you are keeping up with the latest changes and improvements, while continuing to provide the appropriate safety net for you and your family, is always worthwhile.

Your action plan and next steps

☐ Is it time to review your Will and other legal documents or, importantly, to organise them if not done yet?

☐ Have a list of all your important people and where your important documents are kept.

☐ List all the types of life insurance policies you have, including cover you have under superannuation. Review whether they are the right types, whether they provide enough cover and how much you are paying for that cover.

☐ Ensure you have beneficiaries listed for your life insurance cover, especially under superannuation.

☐ As in Chapter 1, make sure you start a savings plan with the first goal to have at least three months of salary saved for a rainy day.

In Chapter 10, I share a full 12-month action plan incorporating many of these actions. In addition, my website (themoneysandwich.com) has plenty of templates, calculators and general information to help you with this process.

The sandwich generation and the older generation

What's in this chapter

The Conversation

Estate planning

Aged care

Seeking financial advice

It's part of your lot as a member of the sandwich generation that you are, by definition, 'sandwiched' between the younger generation (your kids) and the older generation (your parents and/or those of your partner). When it comes to the latter, it's easy, frankly, for old age to creep up without sufficient planning.

Unfortunately, it is not at all uncommon for someone in their 50s to find themselves visiting a parent in hospital after an accident or illness, only to be told that they need to find an aged care place for that parent *right now*. Aside from the trauma around the suddenness of the situation, it inevitably generates a whole host of difficult decision making, both emotional and financial.

A far better and ultimately less stressful way of dealing with this situation would be to prepare for it ahead of time by having what is often called 'The Conversation'. This is a frank conversation held well in advance of an 'old-age emergency' so that if it gets to that point, everyone knows what's expected of them. In this chapter I'll describe what this conversation could look like and what sorts of topics should be included in it. Just as documents like a Will and Enduring Power of Attorney can make life much easier after a family member passes away, having this conversation makes the last years of that person's life far more comfortable, for both the older person and their family.

The big points: The Conversation

What you can do right now, no questions asked

1. Call your parents and ask (tactfully) whether or not they have up-to-date Wills and, if so, where those Wills are kept. (Perhaps tell them you've just updated your own Wills—you have, haven't you?—which prompted you to think about their situation.) Use this conversation as a springboard to organising a time to sit down for a proper conversation on the topics outlined in this chapter.

2. Speak to your siblings, and ensure you are all on the same page with respect to future care for your parents.

3. Decide who will have the Enduring Power of Attorney and Guardianship for your parents as not everyone wants to have this responsibility.

Financial advice for the older generation

One of the awkward situations you can come up against as a financial adviser is being asked by an existing client in, say, their 50s, whether you can provide advice to their parents. It's a common request. After all, clients have built a relationship with their adviser and have come to trust them, so it's only natural that they may like them to advise their parents as well.

Unfortunately, your adviser may tell you that they are unable to help, or at least limited in what they can do. These situations are not straightforward, due to the code of ethics that governs the way financial advisers work. The code prevents advisers working with clients where there may be a perceived conflict of interest with another client, and this extends to those who may benefit from inheriting some or all of the estate of another. This all stems from the government and community wanting to prevent 'elder abuse', which is important. Unfortunately, the code is quite inflexible in terms of what services can be provided.

If you find yourself in this situation, discuss it with your adviser. At the very least they may be able to refer you or your parents to another adviser within the same firm, or to another firm with similar values and a similar approach. Your adviser might also be able to provide some general information if your parents have some fairly simple questions.

The Conversation

You've probably heard the expression, 'You'll have to take me out of here in a box.' You may even have heard it from your own parents. Reality, sadly, often gets in the way of this desire. To put it bluntly, some people outlive their ability to look after themselves at home and necessarily need to move into some form of aged care late in their life.

Rather than pretending this will never happen, it is far healthier, and potentially much less stressful for everyone in a family, if you can have a frank 'What if the worst happens?' conversation ahead of time, just in case.

Believe me, this is much better than being forced to make hasty decisions on the run in an already high-pressure situation.

Let's look at the elements of 'The Conversation'.

Who should be having 'The Conversation', and when?

Ideally 'The Conversation' is something that you and any siblings will have together with your parents. It should happen when everyone is in a good state of mind, and obviously while everyone—especially the older generation—has the mental capacity to be discussing serious matters.

Try not to spring it on your parents. Flag it ahead of time and arrange a suitable time and location. Ideally this won't be the parents' home, where emotional attachment might make the idea of leaving unbearable (and/or it is too easy for Mum to distract herself making tea). Perhaps make an occasion of it—a nice lunch at a quiet restaurant?

Another idea for approaching 'The Conversation' is to start with the estate planning topics—for instance, checking that your parents' Wills exist and are current, and that you all know where the documents are located and who the executors are.

In some cases either you, your siblings or your parents may be uncomfortable with the idea of having this conversation. There can be numerous reasons for this, including the parent-child relationship being reversed or the fear of facing their own mortality.

If this is the case, you could organise a third person to be involved, such as a financial or legal adviser, or simply someone known and trusted by the family of a similar age who will not be a beneficiary of the estate.

It might take several conversations over several months or even years. The important thing is to start 'The Conversation', to bring talking about the future planning of care for your parents/parents-in-law into the present.

Decisions don't have to be made straight away. In fact, early conversations are more about empowering the older generation to have their say about their future.

If you think getting control over your own finances is a challenge, just think about the shift you're asking older people to make, and help them through this.

What to talk about in 'The Conversation'

The overall aim of 'The Conversation' is for everyone to understand the older generation's preferences, both in the best case and the worst case.

We can summarise the main 'agenda' under two main headings: estate planning and aged care. My suggestion is to start with the estate planning side of things and leave the aged care discussion, which can be more emotional, until the end.

Estate planning

Estate planning is fundamentally about managing the transfer of wealth from one generation to the next. There is the legal side of this, in terms of documentation, and there is the financial side. As long as your parents have current Wills, at a minimum, this should be a fairly straightforward discussion.

Legal documents

It's important to check that your parents have their legal paperwork up to date. I'm referring to the documents we discussed in Chapter 6:

- up-to-date Wills

- Enduring Powers of Attorney

- Deeds of Enduring Guardianship (or the equivalent medical decision maker appointment in your state)

- details of any testamentary trusts (if applicable).

It's amazing how many people don't have these things in place. It's surprising how many people don't have a Will, or at least a current one. To reiterate the point made in the last chapter, having a current Will when you die can save your family thousands of dollars in legal fees, let alone the associated heartache — and they don't need to cost a lot of money.

Even less common than Wills are Enduring Powers of Attorney and the appointment of medical decision makers such as Deeds of Enduring Guardianship (in New South Wales). There are other legal options that your lawyer may discuss with you, such as an advance health directive, and so it's worth doing some research before you meet.

Ideally, 'The Conversation' should extend to who has been given what powers, such as executor of the Will, to ensure that everyone involved is comfortable with what's in place. This conversation makes sense and is usually quite straightforward, with few issues. If everyone is comfortable, you may like to move into the specifics of your parents' plans for their assets.

The most likely scenario is that if the husband dies, his estate all goes to his wife, and vice versa. And after the surviving spouse dies, the estate gets split between their children. They may also have a charity or some cause they want their estate to benefit in some way. If possible, it is important to bring such things out into the open. Many instances of family members challenging a Will in the courts occur over such donations that were unforeseen by the family.

More practically speaking (and this is often an issue), does everyone know where the documents are stored and how they can be accessed?

Much of this topic was covered in Chapter 6. While that was aimed at your own estate planning, it all applies equally to that of your parents.

A Memorandum of Directions (MoD)

A Memorandum of Directions (MoD), also known as a 'Letter of Wishes', is becoming a popular way of providing directions and instructions around your estate alongside your Will. An MoD is not a legal document, but it can provide an easy-to-understand overall view for your executors of what your wishes are. It can include more or less anything you want your executors or family to consider or act upon after your death. An MoD can be updated at any time, and added to over time, without the need to visit your legal representative (as in the case of updating your Will).

Finding an estate planning lawyer

With the increasing complexity of baby boomers' estates, it is becoming particularly important to work with a lawyer who specialises in estate planning. An internet search will provide some possibilities, but check also with friends, work colleagues or your existing professional advisers for recommendations.

I prefer to work with someone who has been working in the field for at least three or four years and who is up to speed with the current nuances of estate planning. It should also be looked upon as an ongoing relationship, so make sure you and your parents are comfortable asking questions—even those that feel 'stupid' (but never are).

It's also good to know that the person you are working with is backed up by competent support staff. My own estate planning lawyer fell ill at one point and as he had no backup plan, I was forced to find an alternative when he retired early.

Most modern lawyers, not the old-fashioned type you imagine stuck behind a large mahogany desk, are flexible, empathetic and will come to you if needed. Also, new internet providers such as Your Wills (yourwills.com.au) appeal to those who want a quick and easy option online, and are better than no Will at all.

On this topic, estate planning specialist Tara Lucke (taralucke.com.au) has a number of video blog posts and newsletters on her website that can help you effectively navigate the jargon of this complex subject.

When 'The Conversation' doesn't quite go as expected

Joanna, 60, had two siblings, William and Chris, who were both in their 50s. Their mother, Gwen, now in her 80s, still lived in her own at home and, until very recently, had stayed healthy for her age—'As strong as an ox,' as she always said. She had never shown any interest in discussing her future with her offspring, and the siblings had never felt the need to raise the topic either.

Now, however, Joanna had organised for the four of them to get together at her home. Gwen had slipped over at home recently and, while she didn't break her hip, as many do at her age, the fall did scare her. This time she had sounded quite keen to have a meeting. From various casual conversations, Joanna was aware that her mother's Will and other estate paperwork was up to date. And there had been that one conversation when Gwen had mentioned, almost in passing, a certain aged care facility that she liked the look of, which was near a beach and had a good café nearby.

Now, with the three siblings and Gwen in the room together, they were able to make sure everyone shared Gwen's point of view. Gwen then raised the topic of the family home, saying her preference was for it to be sold after her death and the funds split three ways. Or even sold beforehand if some of the funds were needed to pay for her aged care.

What surprised everyone was William's reaction to this part of the conversation. He objected to the idea of selling the house, saying he never wanted to see the home he was raised in being sold off to some other family. He had never even considered it a possibility. In fact he had always assumed that he and his family would eventually move into the home, as he was the youngest and felt he deserved it for some reason.

William agreed that he could not stop his mother if she decided to sell the home before she died, but he made it clear that he would fight his siblings if they ever tried to sell the place after Gwen's death.

This was the last thing Joanna had expected. She had only ever worried about her mother's wishes. The reality is that issues coming out of left field like this happen all the time, which is why it is so important to have this conversation with all members of the family.

In this situation the solicitor, financial adviser and mortgage broker were able to work out a plan by which William could buy the other two siblings out after their mother's passing, or beforehand if the funds were needed for aged care. The situation was brought under control in plenty of time. It would have been far more problematic if they had never had this conversation and given William the chance to share his thinking.

Aged care

There may be some sensitivities around this topic, as I mentioned, but if circumstances come up that require one or both parents to go into care, would they not prefer to have some say in the matter, while they still can? This can be a challenging part of the conversation, but it does need to happen, and the sooner the better. There are two parts to this topic: your parents' preferences, and what happens to the family home.

What preferences, if any, do your parents have?

Notwithstanding that the facility chosen might be dictated in part by the older person's health (for instance, some facilities specialise in dementia care) or savings available, would they prefer a location close to where they live now? Or would they prefer to be closer to the grandchildren? Or out of the city, near a beach … ? None of this requires choosing a specific facility right now, but it would make choosing one at short notice a lot easier.

There are aged care consultants (along with some websites and apps) who could help you find an appropriate facility and/or assist with the financial aspects of this, but the clearer your parents' preferences are, the easier the task will be for everyone. You never know, this conversation might prompt your parents to visit a few facilities to check them out. At the very least, all of you will have a better understanding of what's in and what's out.

What is to be done with the family home?

Given the home is often a couple's biggest asset and something to which they hold a strong emotional attachment, this is another important topic to raise.

The question is this: if there comes a point where neither parent can live in the home any longer, are they happy for the home to be sold? In particular, are they happy for it to be sold to free up funds to support the costs of aged care, such as to cover an upfront deposit, the cost of the property and/or ongoing care costs? Many people will resist selling their home; some would prefer to lease their house than sell it.

It can be a more emotional question than you might think, which is all the more reason to have this discussion before it becomes critical. Of course, there may be occasions where you have no choice but to sell the house—where there are simply no other funds available to pay for aged care, for instance. But at least if you know your parents' wishes, you and your siblings will be in a better position to make this decision.

One way to make this conversation easier is to acknowledge your parents' preference, if it exists, to stay in their own home right until the end. You might agree that that is everyone's preference, but agree also that if it gets to the point that their doctor advises that one or both should move into a care situation, the doctor's advice will be accepted, even if the parents are not happy with it. Again, having an independent person involved in this discussion can be helpful.

A simple overview of the aged care assessment process

There are three main areas to consider when it comes to aged care assessment.

> ### 1. Needing to be assessed
>
> If and when the time comes, a doctor or someone nominated by an Aged Care Assessment Team (ACAT) needs to assess your parent(s) to determine the level of care needed and any possible subsidy available.

> ### 2. Finding an appropriate aged-care home
>
> You will need to visit a few places to see what's available in the area where your parents would prefer to live. You then need to apply to those you and your parents are interested in. You are not limited to one and can apply to as many as you wish. If the need to find care is urgent and no preparataion has taken place prior, you may need to make a few applications in order to find an available place. Facilities themselves and the myagedcare.gov.au website have information on costs, types of accommodation available and so on.

> ### 3. The finances
>
> Depending on your parents' financial situation, they will need to pay an accommodation contribution or accommodation payment as well as basic daily fees, and other fees depending on the required level of care. For some who cannot fund the care themselves (such as those who don't have a home or other major assets), funding may be provided in full or in part by the government. This woulde require Services Australia to do an assets and income test and provide an assessment.

Importantly, these are major decisions, especially if it may require your parents selling their home, so it is worthwhile seeking specialist advice.

There is plenty of additional information available online regarding aged care. A good place to start is the government's website dedicated to this area, myagedcare.gov.au. In addition, companies like Challenger have plenty of practical information on aged care on their website (challenger.com.au). Also, aged care apps and websites like Care360 (care360.com.au) are also helping people find aged care homes in their area. Finally, if you visit any aged care facility they will have consultants who can take you through the process as well.

Seeking financial advice

There will be times when it is easier for the older generation to be having these sorts of discussions with an impartial third party, such as a financial adviser or solicitor (or, increasingly, both). I've had numerous conversations with retired parents who have preferences they don't feel comfortable expressing to their children. There can be many reasons for this. As one example, I had a client who had one adult son with a mental health issue that made it unrealistic for that son to receive his inheritance as a lump sum. In this situation, we worked with their family lawyer and together were able to create a situation whereby the son would receive an annuity in lieu of a lump sum.

Estate planning and aged care are becoming more and more specialised, so it is worth looking around and ensuring that anyone you or your parents approach has current knowledge and experience in these areas. Just as some lawyers specialise in these areas, some financial advisers are also specialising. See Chapter 10 on how to find an adviser, as those insights will allow you to find appropriate advisers for your parents.

Your action plan and next steps

☐ Understand your parents' wishes when it comes to aged care or their estate. Finding out now by having 'The Conversation' can save unnecessary heartache at a later date for you, your parents and your siblings.

In Chapter 10, I share a full 12-month action plan incorporating many of these actions. In addition, my website (themoneysandwich.com) has plenty of templates, calculators and general information to help you with this process.

Maree's story — I always thought I had time

A client shares the story of her recent experience.

As you get older, you know there will always be responsibility with regard to family, work and finance. However, you always think you'll have time to do everything. I am the perfect example of how that is not the case.

Being an only child, now in her 50s, I've had to take on a lot of the responsibility of caring for my parents. Being married with children doesn't remove that onus from you.

I thought I had time to get everything done for my mother. When we built our home, we built beside my parents. Our thinking was that we wanted them to be a big part of our children's lives, and that in the future being close to them would mean we could help them as they got older.

When my father passed away about 10 years ago, it took a lot out of my mother. However, she was a very independent and fit woman who filled her days with activities. We didn't think much about her estate planning or future care, as I thought we had plenty of time to do this.

That was until one day when I dropped in for my daily visit and found her on the floor, having suffered a heart attack.

She was taken to hospital and from that day on nothing was the same. Things went downhill very quickly. She eventually returned home, but she now needed a nurse every day. She needed all her meals prepared for her, she needed to be bathed and she needed a lot of other help. From being the most totally independent woman I knew, she was now totally dependent on me as her sole caregiver, while I was trying to maintain my career.

Of course, few would have any issue doing this for any parent, as they raised you, you love them and want the best for them. The problem was that I still hadn't seen anyone about my mother's estate planning or getting her finances in order—a situation made worse by the fact that she was now in denial that anything was wrong or that she needed to make a plan for the future.

A few months later, she had a fall. Now it was too late. She was taken to hospital and a few days later I was told by our doctor that she could never return home. She had lost her sense of balance and was also suffering from dementia. She couldn't be left alone, even with help.

I had to now find an aged care home, and quickly.

This was a difficult, time-consuming and expensive exercise. It was a whole new world for me, having to navigate Centrelink, understand foreign aged care terms like RADs and DAPs, and needing to decide whether to sell my mother's house or not. Luckily I had friends who could help, as they had been through this before. Professional advisers and the aged care home provided information as well.

I had also missed my opportunity to arrange an Enduring Power of Attorney as my mother had progressed too quickly with her dementia. Eventually I had to become her financial manager through the government trustee system, which isn't ideal. Having a good solicitor to help with this is crucial.

The government trustee was quite efficient, but it was expensive, as I had to pay $500 for every decision they had to approve to release funds to pay for ongoing aged care. Even if this is just once every year, it adds up.

Organising an Enduring Power of Attorney (and Deed of Guardianship) would have cost a lot less, and would only have needed to happen once.

My lessons from this for anyone with ageing parents is to have the talk with them early about what will need to happen in the future. Get legal advice and other professional financial help, as you don't have to do this all on your own. And make sure you have everything set up long before it is needed, so that the pressure is off you when the time comes.

The sandwich generation and the younger generation

What's in this chapter

Financial literacy for the younger generation

What type of money personality is your child?

Superannuation and the younger generation

Avoiding the debt trap

Supporting a head start

One of the main concerns of couples who come to see me for the first time is seldom their own finances—it's those of their adult or soon-to-be-adult children. Parents are often concerned about their offspring being able to save enough for a deposit to get into their first home, being able to afford to leave home and, in particular, being weighed down by a life in debt.

There is some substance to these concerns. It starts with easy access to loans, which is amplified by widespread advertising, especially on television and the internet, of quick and easy loans for $2000 to $5000. Add to that the promotion of credit cards, interest-free periods and, more recently, 'buy-now-pay-later' products. 'Bad debt', as we defined it in Chapter 2, is easy to come by.

Accruing debt early in life can be debilitating in all sorts of ways. It can create unhealthy financial habits that are hard to shake. It can make it difficult to acquire 'good debt', such as a mortgage. It can even lead to depression or worse.

So teaching your young adults about debt, and particularly the distinction between good and bad debt, is an important part of helping them set up a sound financial future. But it's not just about debt. Teaching good habits around saving and investment are also pieces of this puzzle.

The big points: Setting up your young people

What you can do right now, no questions asked

This section has to start with communication. Get in touch with your kids and tee up a time to speak to them. Perhaps organise lunch together. Use this conversation to:

1. share some of what you've been doing with your finances (you don't need to go into detail—just letting them know that you're getting organised can be enough)

2. tease out *their* attitudes to finance. Are they open to learning more? Do they feel they need advice but don't know where to look? Is money causing them stress?

3. read the section 'What type of money personality is your child?' and see if you can recognise your child's personality and how you could help or at least point them in the right direction

4. tell them what you've been doing on the estate planning front. You might need a separate time to have 'The Conversation'.

Hopefully the result of this conversation will set the wheels in motion for some further and possibly ongoing discussion and identify opportunities for you to help them out if you can (and they're open to it).

Financial literacy for the younger generation

We all want our kids to be smart with their money, and possibly to avoid making the mistakes we did. Creating good habits and getting cash flow under control, minimising bad debt, and looking towards starting to build an investment portfolio, no matter how modest, are all important for the 20-something generation.

The good news is that it's never too late for your adult kids to start learning some basic financial literacy — even if all those great intentions you had when they were younger never amounted to much!

The tricky part is that many young people aren't so keen on taking advice from their parents — on anything. When it comes to financial matters, some simply aren't interested, while others are more focused on earning enough to pay next week's bills.

Financial guidance they might actually listen to

Much of this book — including Chapter 1 on taking control of your money, Chapter 2 on getting to grips with debt and Chapter 4 on building wealth — is relevant at any age, so you might encourage them to have a read of those.

However, I'm a realist, and I acknowledge that the most likely way younger people are going to absorb useful financial information is by hearing it from other young people. There are some wonderful people doing a great job in financial education through podcasts, webinars and various social media outlets. Two well-rated (including by my own adult children and their friends) podcasts, run by people I know, are:

- **She's on the Money** hosted by Victoria Devine

- **My Millennial Money** hosted by Glen James and John Pidgeon

In the meantime, from my own experience with my own young adult children as well as my clients' children, I can summarise my money smart, future ready advice with the following three golden rules (I also have an infographic available on themoneysandwich.com, which your adult children may prefer to read and download).

1. Get your money under control

The number-one issue for most young adults (though this is not limited to this age group) is living 'pay cheque to pay cheque'.

Especially for those who are paid monthly, that last week can be really tough. Setting up a two-account system as described in Chapter 1, whereby you effectively pay yourself a weekly wage into your everyday account (your 'personal expense account'), is a simple way of getting your money under control and starting to build your savings.

The number-two issue is access to too much easy debt. The best option with debt is to have none at all. However, if you do feel the need for a credit card or other forms of debt, aim to never have more debt than you could pay off in 10 months. Never exceed the limit on your credit card provided by the bank: it's in their interest for you to over-extend yourself.

2. Have a hidden fortune for the future

I understand that retirement is a long, long way off, and more than likely not something you are thinking about now. However, the average 25-year-old will have over $1 million in their super when they retire, so it is worth making sure it is invested in a way that is going to provide you with a good return. In most cases this simply means making sure your superannuation contributions are going into your fund's 'high growth' option, not the default 'balanced' option. Once you've done that, you can safely forget about it. In Chapter 4, I explain how with time on your side, the 'high growth' option will more than likely double your super account over 30 years, compared with leaving it in the default balanced option.

3. Set up your safety net now

If you were told that your home had over a 70 per cent chance of burning down in your lifetime, would you insure it? Of course you would. Saying that, the risk of your home burning down is not that high, but in practice the risk of developing some form of cancer, heart condition or stroke over your lifetime is at that level. That being the case, it would be wise to consider taking out some trauma cover (refer to Chapter 6). A good place to start is an amount of cover that would provide one year's salary. You can always increase this later when you have greater responsibilities, including having your own kids.

Why now? Firstly, you never know when you will need it. But secondly, if you take out this insurance now, you can 'lock in' the premium at a constant, or 'level' rate, which will make it much cheaper in later years when you have the greatest chance of claiming.

The other component of your safety net is to put aside the equivalent of three months' salary as a 'rainy day' fund. The experience of the COVID-19 pandemic has demonstrated all too clearly how important this can be. Make it a priority.

Once you have these three areas under control, you can then look forward to 'what's next': saving for overseas holidays, buying your first property or building a share portfolio—or all three.

It's amazing what you can achieve if you have your money under control.

What type of money personality is your child?

Every child (like every adult) tends to have their own relationship to money—what we call their 'money personality'. When it comes to the Black Friday or Boxing Day sales, is your child the type who looks forward to spending up big, credit cards at the ready? Or are they the type who will target something specific and save carefully to take advantage of a good price when it is available?

Understanding, even if roughly, what sort of money personality your children have can guide you in understanding their motivations when it comes to money, and help you help them make good money choices.

In the following sections, I summarise five different money personalities. Most kids will probably be a combination of two or more of these—they are fairly extreme examples—but it's also likely that one type will stand out.

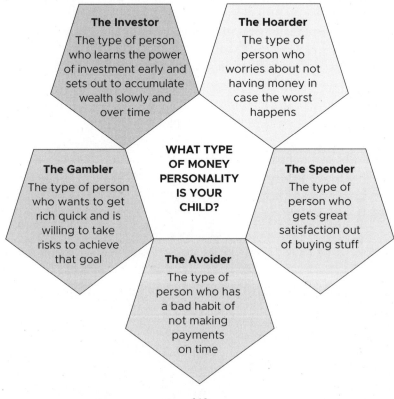

The Investor
The type of person who learns the power of investment early and sets out to accumulate wealth slowly and over time

The Hoarder
The type of person who worries about not having money in case the worst happens

The Gambler
The type of person who wants to get rich quick and is willing to take risks to achieve that goal

WHAT TYPE OF MONEY PERSONALITY IS YOUR CHILD?

The Spender
The type of person who gets great satisfaction out of buying stuff

The Avoider
The type of person who has a bad habit of not making payments on time

The hoarder

This type of person worries about not having money in case the worst happens. They will be good savers, even extreme savers, as they will save even to the extent of avoiding simple luxuries. They would prefer to get shoes repaired rather than buy a new pair (even long after those shoes have reached the end of their useful life). Calling them Scrooge might be going too far, but you get the idea.

With the hoarder, what you should try to understand is why they are so concerned for or fearful of the future that they need such a big nest egg. We all need balance in our lives and, while it's important to save, spending money on holidays and things you would enjoy, within limits, is not unreasonable. If your child is being spooked by negative headlines about falls in the sharemarket, for instance, perhaps spending some time learning about how the market works, and how, historically, it has always performed well in the long term, might set their mind at ease.

The spender

Spenders get great satisfaction out of buying stuff, whether they can actually afford it or not. They see owning goods as exemplifying their doing well or as emphasising their own self-worth. When they buy something, they will often say things like, 'I deserve this.' Many spenders use debt to spend, especially credit cards or easy loans like buy-now-pay-later schemes.

Spenders need to be conscious that if they have the money to spend, they also have the money to save. They could turn their habit to their advantage. On the other hand, if they find themselves at the end of each pay period with nothing left in the bank, they need to understand where their money is going, get some control back and possibly find areas to cut back. This is even more important in the common case of the spender who has a habit of spending more than they earn. In this case they really do need to stop, start paying back their debt and then set some limits for the future. Spenders don't have a problem if they have a balance between spending and saving. Point your child to some of the methods described in Part 1 of this book if they need some guidance.

The avoider

Avoiders, as the name suggests, are those who have a bad habit of not making payments on time. Often they have not kept track of how much they owe to whom, or when their loans are due. They keep telling themselves they are just too busy doing other things to deal with this stuff (whether they are actually busy or just using busyness as an excuse). Avoiders are typically not good at keeping records or doing any form of tracking of their spending that requires financial discipline. Even if the avoider has money, they probably won't invest it, as they're just not interested.

There may be good reasons why the avoider tries to stay clear of financial matters. Perhaps they didn't enjoy maths at school and they see money management as more of the same. Many creative people find the straight logic of money hard to deal with. For some, money just isn't a priority.

Dealing with it comes well down the list after work, social life and family.

Of course, as parents we know that the reality of life is that there will always be things we need to do, even though we don't like doing them. Perhaps encourage them by pointing out how much easier all this money stuff is once you have it under control. And demonstrate that having a good savings habit and building up a nest egg provides a real sense of freedom—and it doesn't need to involve a whole lot of effort. There are those who, once they make a start on controlling their money and understanding it better, find they actually don't mind having to do it, and enjoy the opportunities it creates.

The gambler

The gambler is the person who wants to get rich quick and is willing to take risks to achieve that goal. Whether it is through making speculative high-risk investments or betting on the horses, they always see a big win around the corner. Win or lose, they enjoy the buzz of being involved and the thrill of the ride. Many gamblers enjoy learning about money, but they'd rather learn by doing than by listening to advice.

Of course, most entrepreneurs are gamblers, including those behind some of the biggest success stories. However, what sets the winners apart is that they usually have mentors or advisers around to help them. They understand the benefits of not repeating the mistakes of others. These gamblers don't fall into the trap of the sort of get-rich schemes we always see in the media: the ones that chew up their investors' life savings.

The main concern for the gambler is when their investment strategy turns into gambling and gets out of hand—when their self-worth starts to come from picking winners or taking a punt. Gambling addiction is a major problem in Australia, and it is important that the gambler seeks help if they feel they need it, or even if they don't. Chapter 10 has contact details for help centres if required.

Making speculative investments, and even betting on the races, is fine as long as these form only a small part of your portfolio, or you're spending money you can afford to lose. And of course, the gambler must remember never to put all their money into a single investment, no matter how 'sure fire' it is, nor how big the promised returns are.

The investor

The investor is the child who learns the power of investment early and sets out to accumulate wealth slowly and over time. In many ways they are the opposite of the gambler. This money personality usually enjoys money and the 'art' of investing. They want to manage their investments themselves and enjoy doing so. They probably make a hobby out of it.

There is not much wrong with the investor, as long as they have balance in their life and aren't spending all their time following their investments. We all have only so many hours in the day. Many successful investors still outsource management of their funds in order to free up spare time for themselves and their family.

Superannuation and the younger generation

There is one thing you might strongly encourage your young adults to look at as soon as they can: their superannuation choices. While they probably won't have a significant amount accrued in super yet, it's important that what they do have, and what they continue to accrue over at least the next 20 years, works as hard as possible for them.

As we discussed in some detail earlier, it makes sense for most people to have their superannuation savings invested in the high-growth multi-asset fund offered by their superannuation fund—not the default balanced fund. This is especially the case for younger people, who won't have access to this money for many years.

Choosing the high-growth fund could more than double their superannuation savings by the time they retire.

Life insurance inside super

Life insurance is also provided by superannuation funds on an 'opt-in' basis for under-25s and those with a super balance of less than $6000. My recommendation is that most people in this age group should review the insurance offerings of their super fund and strongly consider opting in. Choosing a relatively low level of life insurance and total and permanent disability (TPD) insurance is likely to save them money in the long term. Refer to Chapter 6 for a more detailed discussion of life insurances.

Avoiding the debt trap

There are two significant factors at play when we consider growing levels of debt among young Australian adults. These factors represent significant societal changes over recent decades.

One is today's widespread expectation of instant gratification, and the other, which both drives and feeds off that, is the easy availability of debt through credit cards, 'interest-free' periods and buy-now-pay-later products.

Research shows that millennials hold an average of around $5000 in credit card debt. The COVID-19 pandemic has only made this worse, with Australian 18- to 34-year-olds three times more likely, according to the CPRC (Consumer Policy Research Centre), to have taken out payday lender loans, credit card debt and other forms of consumer debt during this period.

Of course, as parents there is a limit to how much we can do to prevent our offspring getting into debt. Telling them about the old days when we had to get to the bank before it shut on a Friday afternoon isn't going to cut it.

I would encourage you to pass on some of the information from Chapter 2 on managing debt, especially the difference between good debt (for purchasing 'good' assets like property or shares) and bad debt (for purchasing 'bad' assets, such as luxury cars or boats, that don't provide an income).

All we can really do is lead by example and encourage them to find out for themselves about the risks of debt and how to avoid it.

Supporting a head start

Where those of us in the sandwich generation have always looked at property first and foremost from a lifestyle perspective—we bought a home to live in before we considered buying property as an investment—ever-increasing housing prices have led to a shift in this attitude among those currently in their 20s and 30s. In fact, when it comes to financial matters, surveys we've conducted point to property as the number-one investment area that this age group want to know more about.

From the younger generation's perspective:

- Buying an investment property need not be a significant drag on income because the cost of the property (the mortgage, predominantly) can be offset by rental income.

- Owning an investment property allows them to get into the property market without having to lock themselves into living in any one location.

- Owning an investment property allows them to live more affordably (through renting in their preferred desirable inner suburb, for example).

Helping the younger generation get into property

The biggest barrier to getting into property, whether your own home or an investment, has always been raising the deposit. Thirty years ago a deposit of $20 000 would have been enough to get you started, but now that number is more likely $100 000, if not more. Wages have not grown at anywhere near that level. This is where, depending on your own situation, you might be able to help. There are three main options.

Provide a loan for the deposit against your own home

If your own home is paid off or close to it, you might consider extending a loan to your child for all or part of the deposit on a property by drawing funds against your home, such as via a redraw facility.

Should you go down this path, it is important to formalise the arrangement with a written agreement.

Don't avoid this because you think it suggests a lack of trust in your children; it is important for them to understand the significance of this action, as it is unlikely they have ever made an investment purchase of this size before. This agreement or contract doesn't need to be a complex document, but it does need to cover all the main areas being agreed—including the amount being loaned, the circumstances under which it will be paid back, and how interest will be applied—and it needs to be signed by both parties. It doesn't necessarily require a document drawn up by a solicitor (though this could be done inexpensively). Simple templates can be found online.

While the main reason is to help show your offspring that this is an important step, disagreements over money, while rare, do happen, and they can't be predicted. Don't risk ruining your personal relationship with your offspring by not having a written agreement for any loan you provide them.

Act as guarantor for the deposit

An alternative to providing a loan to your child is to act as guarantor for their deposit.[18] Banks often offer a guarantor structure for this circumstance—that is, for a home loan—that limits the guaranteed amount to just the deposit.

This is different from being guarantor for, say, a business loan. In that case, if the business goes under, you would typically be responsible for the entire loan. In this household deposit situation, if the worst case happened, your child defaulted on their mortgage and the bank repossessed the property, the most you would be up for is the value of the deposit. And in most cases you would expect the value of the property to have grown to cover that amount anyway, after a year or two, and then it can be removed.

Again, any agreement to guarantee a loan should be formally documented.

Co-investment

A third alternative to helping your child into the property market would be to co-invest with them. For instance, it could be that each of you takes a 50 per cent interest in a property. You might put up the full

---

[18] The exact circumstances around acting as guarantor in the way described here vary from one state to another, and between banks. You should seek professional advice and check with your own bank before agreeing to act in this capacity.

deposit at the outset because you have access to those funds, but now instead of that money being a loan, it forms part of your investment.

An arrangement like this can be structured in various ways, including an agreement that the child has the option to buy out your share over time, or that they may pay a higher proportion of the mortgage payments in lieu of rent (assuming they're living in the property).

This can be a relatively simple agreement but one that can benefit both of you. Once again, seeking professional advice would be a good idea, and written formalisation of any agreement is essential.

Joint tenants or tenants in common

If you were to help your child by co-investing with them, or if siblings are buying a property together, then the decision of 'joint tenants' or 'tenants in common' will come up.

This is mainly an estate planning issue dealing with what would happen if either of the owners passes away. With joint tenants, the two parties hold equal shares; if one passes away, their half goes to the other owner. For tenants in common, the relative percentages of ownership can be different, such as 60/40. In addition, if either owner passes away, their share is passed on according to the instructions in their Will.

It's hard to say which is the best option, as it will depend on your circumstances. It usually involves understanding what the long-term plans are for that investment property and whether to sell it or keep it if circumstances change.

A flying start for the grandchildren

While the arrival of your first grandchildren might age you a little more than you expected—not to mention provide a new perspective on the work you did in raising your own kids—making even a modest contribution to their futures can make a huge difference if you get in soon after they are born.

A very popular way of doing this is to start a fund for each grandchild's education, particularly where the intent is for those children to go to private schools. With some schools now costing as much as $30 000 a year—equivalent to close to $60 000 of pre-tax income—there will be many parents who simply can't consider private schooling while also maintaining a high mortgage.

Recall the example in Chapter 3 that showed how compound interest on a regular savings plan, started soon after a child is born, could provide enormous savings on the cost of private school education. In the example, the future cost of school fees was $136 090 but savings of just $70 000 made over 10 years, with interest, was more than enough to cover this cost.

A savings fund of this type can be created via many of the various investment options described in Chapter 4.

There are also dedicated education savings plans on the market, but these tend to offer relatively low returns and they lock the funds in for education only, which reduces their flexibility. Obviously, it's hard to see into the future and it could be risky to assume the choices your children will make about their children's education. Or perhaps you want this fund to support your grandchildren's travel, or their own first home purchase. In this sense, locking funds into a pre-determined outcome is potentially risky.

Personally, I like insurance bonds (refer to Chapter 4) as a tax-effective vehicle for this type of longer-term investment, as these bonds don't place any expectations on what the funds will be used for. The main benefit is that the maximum tax advantage comes from leaving deposited funds in the account for a minimum of 10 years. On the other hand, the funds are accessible with about five to seven days' notice—liquid, but without being so liquid that you could be tempted to withdraw them to solve a short-term challenge.

The 'just in case' conversation

Just as it's important to have 'The Conversation' with the older generation, it's a good idea to take the initiative and have a similar conversation with your offspring. The 'If I wasn't here' checklist in Chapter 6 can act as a good start for this conversation. Once you have all your paperwork in order, simply sit down and go through it all with your adult children, letting them know what you've put in place and where they can find everything.

While many kids hate having this conversation, not wanting to confront the idea that one day you might not be around anymore, if something does happen they will be very thankful that you had your house in order and that they knew about it.

This isn't a conversation that needs to happen frequently, but it's much easier the second time than the first, once the 'taboo' of talking about ageing, illness and death has been broken.

Your action plan and next steps

☐ Understand your own adult children's views on money and debt through the money personality section.

☐ Focus on short-term goals, like savings plans and keeping credit card debt under control.

☐ Get them into money podcasts as a great way to learn and start forming healthy money habits.

☐ Explain how having the right asset allocation mix for their superannuation (such as high growth), for the long term, can help provide a small fortune later.

☐ If buying a property is being considered, discuss ways you might be able to assist. Make sure they follow the rules for buying property (Chapter 4), whether the purchase will be an investment or a home.

☐ Encourage them to lock in some basic life and trauma insurance now at level rates. This will save them significant money in the long term.

In Chapter 10, I share a full 12-month action plan incorporating many of these actions. In addition, my website (themoneysandwich.com) has plenty of templates, calculators and general information to help you with this process.

You can't spend it if you're dead — the importance of wellbeing

What's in this chapter

Quiet time

Read

Exercise

Sleep

Diet

Staying positive

Staying motivated

I've noted a number of times in this book the extent to which money challenges can contribute to stress levels. Feeling out of control of your financial situation, living with high debt, dealing with health problems that threaten your income (especially if you're inadequately insured), worrying about your children struggling with debt or being unable to establish themselves financially…all these things can increase your stress. And in a circular way, financial stress can make many of these problems worse. It's far easier to deal with a major health scare if you know your financial future is safe.

All that said, the best financial situation in the world isn't much use to you if you're living an overly stressful lifestyle. Although I work in finance, I've long understood that a person's financial position is only part of the equation of their wellbeing. Staying mentally and physically healthy, maintaining a positive outlook and getting the balance between work and 'life' right are all critical. I'm always amazed that so many people feel a greater responsibility to their employer than to their family or health.

The bottom line is this: you can't spend it if you're dead, so look after yourself.

This is why when I work with my clients, I try to understand them as people, not just as clients with whom I'm undertaking a transaction. I want to know about their goals, hopes and dreams, the things that keep them up at night, whether they are financial or otherwise. This makes my relationship with them about so much more than the singular dimension of helping them to plan their finances.

In this chapter I want to briefly share some of what I've learnt along the way in terms of maintaining my own wellbeing, along with family and close friends who are always your best support. I don't claim to be an expert or even to have any special knowledge in any of these areas, other than my own experiences, but those experiences are of a professional who just turned 60 and is facing many of the same challenges you might be.

Hopefully this information will prompt you to think about your finances as part of a holistic view of your overall wellbeing, and to look further into any of the described areas that are of particular interest.

Quiet time

Until very recently, I spent a number of years as National President of the Association of Financial Advisers, a national organisation that represents financial advisers and their clients. A large part of our role involves lobbying governments and regulators when it comes to policy and legislation around financial planning. My term in this role coincided with a royal commission into banking that put a bright spotlight on the finance industry. Needless to say, it was a stressful time, especially in the aftermath, as a number of our members lost their businesses under new laws that also made our lives a lot more complicated.

I'm hardly alone. So many people in their 40s, 50s, and 60s find themselves doing stressful work or having other sources of stress in their lives. Of course, we'll never get rid of stress altogether—having some level of stress can be a good thing—but you need to have it under control, understand it and be able to deal with it.

For a long time, I have made a point of finding regular quiet time for myself. Just 10 or 20 minutes to sit in nature on my own, at least every couple of days. I have a favourite tree in North Sydney that I used to sit under between dropping my girls at school and going to work. Fifteen minutes spent just taking in the view across Sydney Harbour calmed the mind and set me up for the day. I'll do something similar anytime I find myself beside the ocean—even between meetings. It is a simple but powerful way of keeping my stress under control, and it became even more important during my time doing both the Association role and my normal day job.

There are numerous ways of doing this, both structured and more casual. Meditation and mindfulness have become increasingly popular in recent years, and they are now available to everyone very easily via various apps you can download to your phone. A 10-minute guided meditation every day can make a huge difference to your ability to cope with stress. Of course 'in-person' sessions of meditation or yoga are even more powerful.

The point is that you need to do something, whether first thing in the morning or before you go to sleep, to just enjoy some quiet time.

Read

I was a kid who loved comic books (*The Phantom* and *MAD* were my favourites), and my dad was happy with that. He definitely held the view that as long as I was reading something, that was a good thing. The proviso was that by the time I was 12 and at high school I had to have read a minimum of five books of his choosing. These included famous titles such as *Moby Dick*, *The Three Musketeers* and *Call of the Wild*. Ever since, I have had a love affair with reading and have tried to pass this on to my children, as my wife also enjoys reading.

I have discovered there are significant benefits to regular reading, including mental stimulation, relaxation, better memory and improved sleep. It's also just enjoyable.

My preferred reading material is fiction, especially action novels, as I find these provide relaxation and the fun of another place in the world. I don't mind a good biography or two as well, my favourites being those of Jimmy Cagney and Howard Hughes. I don't tend to read many technical non-fiction books (apart from marketing and finance books to help my work), but each to their own.

Google may have largely replaced reading as a source of information, but to my mind it is still books that provide knowledge—and enjoyment.

Exercise

Early in 2019 I had surgery for a heart condition I'd known about for a number of years. Obviously this was going to be a fairly serious operation, so it was important that I was in good physical shape going into it.

Not everyone in their 50s is going to have such obvious motivation to get fit and keep their weight under control, but the truth is that the older we get, the greater the likelihood is of health challenges arising. And the best way of being ready for those challenges is to have a reasonable underlying level of fitness.

The exercise approach that has always worked best for me is getting involved in a team sport, in my case football (soccer). Training and playing with a team of blokes (go St Michaels!) has given me a reason to push through any resistance and turn up whenever I can, knowing I am going to have a game of football, and that win or lose there'll always be a beer afterwards. We seem to spend as much time talking afterwards as we do on the field. It is something to look forward to and is almost fitness by stealth.

Football works for me. For you it might be tennis or golf or another sport. Perhaps taking part in organised fitness classes with a friend, or walking with a group, is your thing. Perhaps you're one of that small group who find motivation on their own. Whatever works for you. The important thing is that you're getting off the couch and doing some form of regular exercise, and keeping that up as you move through your 50s and into your 60s. As life expectancies increase, we want to make sure we are maintaining quality of life, not just quantity.

Sleep

It wasn't so long ago that time management experts were encouraging us to squeeze a few more minutes into the start and end of each day in order to get a bit more done…at the expense of sleep. The science of sleep has advanced substantially in recent years and its importance is now recognised as critical to almost every aspect of our health and wellbeing.

I used to be a night owl, regularly staying up until one or two o'clock in the morning, especially on weekends. What I now know is:

- Eight hours of sleep each night — neither too much less *nor* too much more — makes a huge difference to your health.

- You'll get even better results if one to two of those hours is before midnight.

Scientists distinguish between deep sleep and lighter REM sleep, which both play different roles in the recovery that sleep provides. Most of the deep sleep occurs in that period either side of midnight, so if you short-change yourself on that, you'll be missing out on some of the greatest benefits of sleep, even if overall you're getting enough sleep time on the clock.

I've also improved my sleep by avoiding late-night snacks, avoiding drinking (other than water) in the two or three hours before bed and making sure I get off the computer and other devices for at least an hour before bed as well. Of course, these are my aims, and I'm definitely not perfect, but I am trying.

A lot of what I have learnt about the importance of sleep, gut health and fasting has come from mindfulness and meditation coach Chelsea Pottenger of EQ Minds (eqminds.com)—well worth a look.

Diet

Getting our diet right seems to become increasingly more challenging as we get older. Even maintaining the same diet can lead to weight gain as we don't need as much food to sustain ourselves as we used to—particularly if the amount of exercise we do drops off.

Like so many, I have had a not-so-healthy appreciation of junk food, sweets and meat—all things we are told we should be eating less of. And I'm allergic to seafood, so eating more fish—which they tell us we should be doing—isn't an option for me. My saviour, if that's what we can call it, was discovering the Mediterranean diet after our family hosted an Italian exchange student, Alfredo, a decade ago.

Ever since, we have regularly spent time around the Mediterranean, often staying with his family and experiencing the way they eat. In the early days I didn't think I would survive eating as little meat as they tend to eat in those countries, but I soon adjusted to the almost vegetarian diet of pasta and salads—with fat coming from olive oil rather than butter—relatively little sugar, and certainly little in the way of processed foods. They also tend to eat smaller portions than we do. I still hanker for a good steak whenever we get home from one of those trips, but there's no doubt that a more moderate approach to red meat consumption has been good for me.

Other aspects of diet that have worked for me have been the so-called 16–8 intermittent fasting diet and applying some of what I've learnt about gut health.

The *16–8 intermittent fasting* approach to eating is based on restricting your daily food consumption to an eight-hour period, say between 11 am and 7 pm. In my case this translates to a late-morning brunch and an early dinner, and not consuming anything other than water and kombucha (and occasionally—and unofficially!—a glass of red wine) overnight. The idea of this approach that appeals most to me is not to starve yourself—I definitely eat two substantial meals every day, and I don't feel hungry at any point. And if I need to break this pattern I will. For instance, if I am going to be doing physical work, or it's the weekend, I will have breakfast. I always enjoy a good eggs benedict on a Saturday or Sunday. But if I'm just going to be at the computer all morning, that breakfast can wait.

You can find an enormous number of resources on this topic on the internet. I am also kept motivated and held accountable by one of my closest friends, Victoria Black, a wonderful lady who runs Super Fast Diet (superfastdiet.com), helping others like myself who find it hard to do it on their own.

Staying positive

It might sound overly simplistic, but having a positive outlook on life can make a big difference to your health. Think this won't work for you…you've been a pessimist all your life? Think again. There are programs built around mindfulness and happiness that can turn almost any naysayer into a much more optimistic soul.

I recommend everyone watch Shawn Achor's TED Talk, 'The Happy Secret to Better Work'. He points out that most people have things the wrong way round. We tend to believe that when we reach some target—get the dream job, get a salary increase, and so on—this will finally make us happy. Whereas it should be the other way round. Be happy first, *then* you will find it easier to achieve your goals, targets, find the right job, and so on.

A blog I like to keep up with ever since I heard the guys speak at a conference a few years back is *Future Crunch* (futurecrun.ch). They have a way of making science and the future seem fun, and with a very positive and optimistic outlook. It's great to see good news for a change!

Personally I've always tended towards the 'glass half full' outlook on life anyway. I learnt early on to try and have a positive attitude around my daughters and to seek out positivity by enjoying regular good laughs with friends and colleagues. I avoid negativity where I can. If I'm browsing the news on the internet I make a point of never scrolling 'below the line' into the comments section—almost inevitably a source of depressing gloom. And I coach myself to try not to worry about those things I can't control. If you can't control it, why worry about it?

Staying motivated

Of course, the thing that sits behind everything I've talked about so far, in this chapter and in fact in the whole book, is motivation. If you can't find the motivation to manage your money, you're unlikely to spend any time and effort doing so. If you can't find the motivation to eat well, exercise or get enough sleep, you're unlikely to do those things either. (There's a bit of a vicious circle there, for failing to look after yourself tends to reduce your motivation to look after yourself. But that's a bigger topic and beyond my expertise.)

I am a big advocate of having someone in your life who keeps you accountable.

It may be a number of people. But we shouldn't assume that we will be able to motivate ourselves. The top sportspeople, even in individual sports like tennis, still have coaches. So do the most successful business people. If you can find a coach or coaches that will work for you, they will almost certainly be worth the investment. So if you're going to sign up to a gym, pay the extra money and get a trainer, or at least find a gym buddy who'll motivate you to turn up with them. Likewise when it comes to your finances, you need a coach too—especially if you're someone who does not enjoy that aspect of your life.

10

It doesn't end here: Next steps and the importance of advice

What's in this chapter

The next 12 months

Finding and working with a financial adviser

Where to turn if money matters get out of control

If you have read this far, I trust you're feeling somewhat more comfortable about the path ahead as you move towards Year R.

What you need to consider now is whether or not you want to manage everything we've talked about here on your own or find a professional to help you.

My aim with this book has been to give you the tools and knowledge you need to get the basics right and under control—for yourself, your adult children and your elderly parents.

You should now be able to get a lot more out of your savings, insurance and superannuation and look towards a more comfortable life post-Year R, as well as set yourself and your family up to be able to deal with both the unexpected and expected (eventually) disruptions that life throws at us.

The next 12 months

If your aim is to implement the strategies I've shared throughout this book, you shouldn't try to do this all in one go. It's much simpler to focus on specific steps and complete them before moving on to the next one as it's easier to manage. And you'll need to spend some time locating and organising various documents and information.

Here is a guide on how we help our clients get started—the quick and easy things to do initially, through to what will take more time and effort, and then a simple review process.

Importantly if you're not using the services of a professional, find someone like a mentor, who you trust and feel comfortable with, and with whom you would be willing to share what you are doing and trying to achieve, to keep you on track. It should be someone who is willing to listen, provide feedback and be with you for this journey.

First 3 months

- **A goals plan** (Chapter 3): Write down on a piece of paper your three to five major goals. They can be split between short-term goals, such as paying off debt, and long-term goals, such as closing your retirement gap. Importantly, place this somewhere where you can see it regularly, review it and not forget it.

- **Get control of your cash** (Chapter 1): Use the template on our website to understand where your money is going each month and to categorise your expenses.

- **Banking** (Chapter 1): Set up separate bank accounts and, if needed, start paying yourself a weekly 'salary' if paid monthly, for example.

- **A savings plan** (Chapter 1): Start a savings plan, with a regular amount at first that you won't miss. Pay yourself first (set up a transfer to your savings account) at the beginning of each month or pay period.

- **Debt** (Chapter 2): Review what you owe, whether that's credit card debt, loans or mortgages. List what debt you have and at what interest rates, and how much you can afford to pay back and how quickly, to ensure you have this under control as soon as possible.

- **Superannuation** (Chapter 5): List how many super funds you have, which options those funds are invested in (should you be considering high growth for example? — Chapter 4). Check what insurances you have within your fund (Chapter 6) and make sure you nominate a beneficiary.

- **Insurance** (Chapter 6): In addition to insurance under your super fund, list what other life insurance policies you have. Determine whether you have enough cover for you and your family. Use the calculator on our website to help work out how much cover you may need.

3 to 6 months

- **Review:** Go over what you have done in the first three months, what's worked and what hasn't, and what needs to be looked at or tweaked in the next period.

- **Cash flow** (Chapter 1): There will be expenses that are one-offs that may have been missed in your initial review of your expenses. You may need to average these out so you can have sufficient funds for the next time this one-off bill arrives.

- **Banking** (Chapter 1): If you are starting to build up some savings, it may be time to set up a third bank account that offers a higher interest rate.

- **A savings plan** (Chapter 1): If you haven't missed what you have been putting away for savings, it may be time to slightly increase this. If the opposite is true, you may need to reduce your monthly savings amount. It's important to just tweak this rather than stop altogether.

- **Debt** (Chapter 2): If you now know how much you owe, and you are paying down regularly, review whether or not you could tweak this to possibly pay off more debt.

- **Superannuation** (Chapter 5): This will be your major asset for post-Year R, so it's worth spending some time working out whether you are on track for a comfortable retirement or not. If you have already reviewed how your super is invested, you can use our website's calculator or Moneysmart's calculator to work out what your retirement gap is. You don't need to do anything just yet unless you have spare funds or salary, but it's important to know so you can address this in the future when you are ready.

- **Insurance** (Chapter 6): Have you had your life insurance policies for a number of years without review? Like most things, life insurance policies change and can become more competitive in premiums and benefits, so they're worth checking.

- **Estate planning** (Chapter 6): It's time to organise a Will or have it reviewed, especially if you've not done so in the last, say, five years. You want to have a say in what happens to your assets when you die rather than have the government step in and charge your estate thousands more than is needed.

6 to 12 months

- **Review:** Go over what you have done in the previous three months. What's worked and what hasn't, and what needs to be looked at or tweaked in the next period?

- **Cash flow** (Chapter 1): You should start to see real changes in your attitudes and understanding of your cash flow by now. Whether you have made any significant changes, you at least understand what you are spending your money on each month. You then have control to plan what changes you may want to make now or in the future.

- **A savings plan** (Chapter 1): Continually tweak this and look for other opportunities, such as tax refunds or increases in salary, that can help increase your savings. Once you have more than a few thousand in your savings account, if your goals are medium to long term, you should start considering higher growth types of investment. Consider using a wrap account or an investment bond (Chapter 4) to potentially get your funds growing faster over time.

- **Debt** (Chapter 2): After a year, some or all of your credit card debt should be paid off or at least under control, and you should have a plan for the future. Once paid off, you should only keep one, maybe two, credit cards for emergencies.

Every 12 months

- **Review:** Go over what you have done in the previous year, what's worked and what hasn't, and what needs to be looked at or tweaked in the next year.

- **Checklist:** Every year, you should have a checklist to go through covering all the areas discussed here (I also provide an Annual Review checklist at themoneysandwich.com). For some areas, nothing will need to be done as things are going well and on target. In other areas, such as life insurance, a proper review every two to three years is warranted.

- **Goals** (Chapter 3): Check your initial list. Has it changed? Once some targets are reached, you may need to set new goals and update your goals list. Again, make sure you keep it somewhere where it can be seen and not forgotten.

- **Year R** (chapters 3, 4 and 5): You need to review your retirement gap each year to see whether you are on target or your plan needs to be tweaked. This could involve extra salary sacrifice contributions, for example, to help bridge the gap.

- **Your adult children and elderly parents** (chapters 7 and 8): Now that you have had a year to get comfortable with your own financial position, it is worth seeing how you can help your children get into good money habits. Can you recognise what types of money personality they are? Also, see whether your parents need help with aged care or estate planning as they reach the next stage of their lives.

- **Educate yourself:** If you're not working in the finance industry, it's hard to keep up with ongoing superannuation changes or what's happening in the sharemarket on a daily basis. Still, it's worth trying to self-educate and keep up to date with what's happening.

Knowledge is power, and that comes through education.

Anything else?

Remember to review how much time all this financial stuff is taking you as you need to ensure you keep a healthy work-life balance. One of the main aims of this book is that control of your money and finances should help reduce the everyday stress and anxiety that money issues can cause.

It may also help if you have a mentor, friend or someone you trust to run all this by each year as it's tough to do all on your own.

Best of luck with this. Once you start getting into a regular habit of reviewing and tweaking, with someone helping you to stay accountable, it is amazing what you can achieve. On the other hand, I do suggest you only take all this on 'solo' if you're really interested in it and have the time.

Finding and working with a financial adviser

The alternative to doing it yourself is to work with professional advisers — a financial adviser, an accountant and a lawyer/legal adviser at a minimum — to help you manage what we've discussed in this book.

There are a number of reasons for seeking professional advice. First, most of us lead busy lives, which means everything needs prioritising.

In my experience, unless you are really dedicated to 'the money stuff' it just won't happen, even with the best intentions.

Second, this stuff is complicated. Even those of us who spend our lives at the coal face of financial matters can struggle to keep up with constant changes in the financial markets, financial product offerings and legislation (especially around superannuation). Like health professionals, the job of financial and legal advisers is to stay up to date and ensure their clients achieve the best outcomes based on current circumstances.

Third, don't you have better things to do? Think about all the important things in life: your health, your relationships, your spirituality/religion, your career, your recreational activities, your wealth, and your legal and insurance protections. Of all these, only the management of your wealth and estate through legal advice and life insurances can be outsourced. Having someone else look after those things takes them off your plate so you can get on with enjoying your life.

Finally, advisers do more than just provide advice and management of the day-to-day stuff. They can also act as a coach. We all need coaches to keep us accountable and on track, whether we're talking about our health or our money. There's no point having a plan if there is no action to put it into place.

Having people to keep you accountable in life generally, let alone in your financial matters, is just as important as having a plan.

Simply, I'm suggesting seeking advice because from my experience I know it is the most effective way to make sure the essentials get done, you stay on track and that you get the best results.

Finding an adviser

The best way to find a financial adviser is to get a recommendation from someone who has an adviser and is happy with their experience. Failing that, there are a number of websites and associations that can help. Here are a few suggestions, most of which have a 'find an adviser' function. You can search for advisers who are in your area and those with particular specialties, such as aged care, insurance or retirement planning.

1. **Association of Financial Advisers (AFA):** afa.asn.au

2. **Financial Planning Association (FPA):** fpa.com.au

3. **Adviser Ratings website:** adviserratings.com.au

4. **Financial Advice (for New Zealand):** financialadvice.nz

5. **ASIC Moneysmart website (for Australia):** moneysmart.gov.au.
   Live Sorted (for New Zealand): sorted.org.nz.

   These sites include financial adviser registers on which you can find government information on potential advisers, including their history of work and qualifications.

If you are not getting a specific recommendation, I suggest you pick two or three advisers who you feel may suit you and visit each of them. Make sure you understand a potential adviser's fee structures and how they invest your money, but make sure also that you feel a level of connection with this person. Ideally, your choice will be the start of a long and prosperous relationship for you and your family, so it's worth looking around until you find someone you feel comfortable with.

If you want to get down to the detail of what you should expect, the best way is to go to the ASIC Moneysmart website as it has a comprehensive amount of information on this as well as questions to ask your adviser.

Preparing to meet an adviser

Preparation is key. Before you meet a financial adviser:

1. **You need to know why you want a meeting.** Is it to see what your retirement gap is (refer to Chapter 3), so you know how much money you will need post-Year R? Is it to review how your investments and super are invested and make sure you are getting the best out of them? Is it for tax planning, to create an investment strategy, to plan the purchase of that investment property on the beach? Whatever the reason, it is good to go in with two or three key objectives.

   Remember, a good adviser will ask plenty of questions and may help you come up with other goals, but it is much better to think about what you want out of the meeting before it takes place.

2. **You need to have all your basic financial information ready.** You may even need to provide it before the meeting, so you can make the best use of your time in the meeting rather than spending it trying to work out your super balances, insurance cover, and so on.

3. **You should have plenty of questions to ask at the meeting.** Especially in finance, there is no such thing as a stupid question. Look on your experience with an adviser as being about their teaching you as well as advising you. The days of blindly following the advice of anyone, let alone an adviser, are long gone. Make sure you are prepared to fully understand what is being explained and ready to thoroughly explore areas you have heard about and want more information about.

Meeting a financial adviser for the first time

When you're ready to meet your adviser for the first time, keep in mind the following:

1. **Even if an adviser has been recommended to you, this is no guarantee they will be the right fit for you.** You may need to meet two or three advisers before you feel comfortable with someone. Most initial meetings are free, as they are really about getting to know each other. This works both ways: the adviser may feel they are not well equipped to help you, perhaps because their specialities aren't a good match for what you're looking for.

2. **Before the meeting starts, they will provide you with a range of documents, including their Financial Services Guide (FSG).** (They may have emailed this to you before the first meeting.) This guide is important, as it provides some essential background information on the adviser, their education, experience, their licensee, and so on. I would not continue with the meeting if you have not been provided with this.

3. **By the end of the first meeting, the adviser should have a good understanding of what your financial and broad life goals and objectives are.** They should have asked enough questions about you and your situation to provide some feedback as to what types of services they can provide, and how complex or comprehensive their advice may need to be.

4. **Hopefully, you will walk away from that first meeting (or at least one of them) feeling confident you have met someone you can work with and build a relationship with.** In particular, you need to feel this person has avoided baffling you with technical jargon; instead, explaining concepts in an easy-to-understand fashion. They will likely have provided you with some rough ideas or options to consider.

5. **Depending on the adviser, most provide a summary of the meeting to ensure that any information you have supplied was captured**

correctly and that your goals have been clearly understood. The adviser will detail what services they can provide and the associated costs. All of this is important, as the initial plan is just the start. What your adviser will do going forward to keep you accountable is just as important.

Proceeding with your new adviser

After your meeting, if you are comfortable and you think you have found the right adviser to move forward with, there's a little initial admin to take care of first:

1. **The adviser will probably need some more detailed information from you, including having you complete a risk profile (similar to the one in Chapter 3).** They will need various authorities from you to allow them to access and research the status of your existing super, investment and insurances, depending on what services you have indicated you want to proceed with.

2. **Once the adviser has all the information they need, they will complete a report called a 'Statement of Advice', or SoA.** This will include your details, their understanding of why you need advice (such as filling a retirement gap) and their proposed solutions and recommendations, including investment strategies (based on your risk profile) and possible product suggestions. They will detail reasons why these have been recommended, as well as associated fees, both upfront and ongoing. They will also include any other pertinent information that needs to be disclosed.

   The *Statement of Advice* is a long document and needs to be carefully reviewed. Hopefully they will have included a summary at the beginning. Your adviser should also go through the document with you at a subsequent meeting. Understand that advisers operate under strict compliance conditions and need to make sure they don't miss anything. If the SoA appears confusing, that is not intended.

A good adviser will take the complexity out of the Statement of Advice and answer any questions you may have using simple language, so that you ultimately feel confident that you understand it.

3. **If you agree to proceed from this point, you will sign an 'Authority to Proceed' and the adviser will start the implementation process (assuming that is part of the plan you have agreed to).** There is never any compulsion for you to implement the plan with the adviser who provided it to you. You are quite within your rights to do this yourself if you are confident in doing so. That said, the adviser is likely the best person to implement your plan, as they have made the recommendations and thoroughly understand everything they have suggested. Further, they will ensure their recommendations are fully implemented — not lost under other priorities.

Ongoing advice and service

Early on, your adviser should map out what services they will provide under an ongoing service arrangement. These could include regular meetings or contacts, with a minimum of an annual review. They might monitor investments on your behalf or actively re-balance your investments in line with an agreed plan, along with numerous other potential services. Importantly, they should always be ensuring that you are on track to reach whatever goals and objectives you specified in your initial meeting.

Many people feel these ongoing aspects of a financial planner's service are unnecessary, that once you have a plan you can take it all over yourself.

From many years' experience, my view is that while many people are perfectly capable of doing this themselves, it ends up being like most new year's resolutions: there's great enthusiasm for a few months, but that eventually peters out, leaving the plan neglected.

Having someone else, your adviser in this case, on hand to keep you accountable and on track is usually worth the money. Then you can get on with your own life, safe in the knowledge that the money stuff is being looked after. (An advantage of web-based accounts these days is that you can have the best of both worlds. You can leave the 'doing' to your adviser while being able to check up at any time and see how your investments are going.)

Understanding the fees

Fees for financial advice are typically made up of two components: a one-off fee for the Statement of Advice (and, potentially, its implementation), and ongoing service fees for the maintenance of your financial affairs.

In paying fees for financial advice, you are paying for the time and expertise of your adviser, in return for the value of the services they are providing to you. In the same way that we might be willing to pay thousands of dollars for a medical procedure because of the quality of life that procedure will provide, paying for financial advice provides value in terms of making your life easier. Financial advice also provides direct value, in that it will more than likely lead to better returns on your investments than you would achieve on your own.

While the fees associated with financial advice may seem high in dollar terms, they need to be kept in perspective. If you are looking at advice ahead of your retirement, you only get one shot at retiring comfortably and ensuring your funds last your lifetime. Getting your finances right could mean you have tens of thousands of dollars more to draw on over the longer term. In that light, the fees associated with advice are actually quite small. I'm confident that any well-regarded adviser will provide you with good value over time.

One-off fees

One-off fees for the Statement of Advice and implementation can range anywhere between $2000 and $6000 depending on the levels of options and the complexity of the plan. Different advisers charge in different ways, but like anything in life they must demonstrate the value they are providing, and you need to decide whether that value is there for you.

To give you some understanding of what goes on behind the scenes, the average plan takes an adviser around 10 to 30 hours to complete, including meetings, research and coming up with strategies and recommendations. Based on a typical hourly rate of $200 per hour, you can start to see where the costs accrue.

Ongoing service fees

Ongoing service fees range, on average, between $3000 and $10000 per year, though they can be higher depending on the complexity of your financial affairs.

The value of service fees lies in access to your adviser's expertise, the time they free up for you in not having to micro-manage your finances, and/or their keeping you accountable for ensuring that your affairs are kept in order. These things combined can add hundreds of thousands of dollars to the value of your retirement assets, of which the service fees will likely be a relatively small proportion.

For a 50-year-old, a good financial adviser might mean the difference between retiring with $1.5 million in assets compared with $900000. If the cost of this advice was $6000 per year over 15 years (so $90000 in total), the return on that investment should be self-evident.

Ongoing service fees might be higher in the first year due to the higher level of intervention and contact/education required. They will normally level out after that. All this will be explained in the Statement of Advice.

The way of fee charging in last 10 years has been evolving. Previously many advisers were charging based on a percentage, so if it was 1 per cent for example, on a super fund account balance of $600000, then the fee would be $6000, or $10000 if the account balance was $1000000. More advisers are now charging a flat ongoing fee based on work done or value provided as it's not just about their super but a more holistic approach and how it fits in with their post-Year R plans.

In some cases, options will exist to pay some or all of the ongoing fees out of your superannuation, or some of them may be tax deductible. If so, all of this should be explained to you.

Advisers operate today under strict legislation that ensures that you, the client, are in control of the relationship. As such, fees will never be imposed on a 'set and forget' basis. You will need to sign off on any ongoing fees on an annual basis. You can also 'switch off' the fees at any time. In short, there are plenty of safeguards in place if you ever feel you are no longer receiving value for the money you are paying your adviser.

Commissions on investment products

Until 2013, financial advisers were also able to earn some or all of their income from so-called 'trailing commissions', whereby they were paid an ongoing commission for the sale of investment products to their clients, for as long as the client maintained those investments. Changes to the laws governing financial advice saw those commissions phased out since then, and they are no longer able to form part of the fees associated with financial advice. The only exception today is life insurance products.

The removal of these arrangements was undoubtedly a good thing for consumers who were not previously getting advice, but those who were, and who preferred that arrangement, were not given a choice and needed to switch to the fee-based system regardless.

Advisers can now earn commissions only on life insurance products, and such arrangements are highly transparent, including being declared in the Statement of Advice.

Taking action if things go wrong

Unfortunately, it is possible that things can go wrong in the relationship between you and your financial adviser. This is rare. Statistics from the Australian Financial Complaints Authority (AFCA) show that the number of complaints in financial advice is one of the lowest among all professions, including medical and legal. Nevertheless, there are safeguards in place to provide you with help if it is needed.

Your adviser's Financial Services Guide (FSG) will lay out how to make a complaint if you need to. If you've lost the copy the adviser gave you in your first meeting, ask them to send it to you again. An adviser must respond to a complaint within a specific time period, and hopefully their response will settle the matter. If you do need to take things further, AFCA—formerly the Financial Ombudsman Service—is a free, independent service.

In the worst case—if you suspect money has been stolen from you, for example—you can contact the industry watchdog, the Australian Securities and Investments Commission (ASIC), or simply go to the police.

Where to turn if money matters get out of control

If you're feeling overwhelmed by money or personal issues, it can feel like you are on your own and that the world is against you. It is important to know there are many government-run and not-for-profit services available to provide you with assistance.

Financial counsellors, such as The National Debt Helpline (see the next section for contact details), provide a free, confidential and valuable service and should be applauded for the great work they do for those in need. They can provide help and assistance on all areas of money, such as trouble paying bills or tax—or worse, once debt collectors are involved.

Many financial advisers also provide pro-bono services to charities and should be encouraged to do more, wherever possible.

If you need help with debt

Call the National Debt Helpline on 1800 007 007, or visit ndh.org.au. The free telephone helpline is open Monday to Friday, 9.30 am to 4.30 pm. For New Zealand, MoneyTalks is a free and confidential advice service on 0800 345 123, or visit moneytalks.co.nz.

If you need help with expenses, including food

There are numerous charities and community groups that provide support to those in need of essential goods, such as food and clothing (for school, for example). Some can also assist with the payment of utility bills, such as for electricity and water.

Here are some organisations you can contact:

- Salvation Army, on 13 72 58

- St Vincent de Paul Society, on 13 18 12

- your local council, community centre, church or community organisation.

The Department of Social Services has a comprehensive Grants Service Directory online at serviceproviders.dss.gov.au.

If you need personal and emotional support

Help is also available for any type of serious personal issue or crisis. Here are some free services available to you or anyone you feel may need help:

- For gambling issues, contact Gambling Help Online on 1800 858 858 or gamblinghelponline.org.au

- Crisis support is available from Lifeline on 13 11 14, lifeline.org.au

- For help with depression or anxiety, contact Beyond Blue on 1300 22 46 36 or beyondblue.org.au.

Pino and Rita's story — all advisers are not the same

Pino and Rita were in their early 50s, and Pino was keen on getting some financial advice. In the past, Pino had received some great help from his accountant, but with his small but growing business, he saw the benefits of seeking more specialised help. At their last meeting, his accountant had suggested that now he was starting to make a good profit, he should start getting his own personal finances in order, especially with a young family.

Rita was hesitant about seeking advice as she thought it would be expensive; however, she agreed to meeting a couple of advisers to see what they had to offer.

Meeting with Adviser 1

The couple met with an adviser who took them through a fairly detailed analysis of what their situation was and what they wanted for the future.

A few days later, the adviser sent them a letter of engagement with a summary of the meeting, setting out their present situation and outlining some basic strategies and options to consider.

The adviser wrote that the next step, should Pino and Rita wish to proceed, would be the drawing up of some more detailed advice in line with their goals, in the form of a Statement of Advice (SoA) report.

The SoA would include:

- ways of paying down the mortgage

- increasing their insurances to a more appropriate level

- more diversification of their investments

- working out what savings they needed to accrue in order to be able to retire at age 65.

This all sounded good to Pino and Rita. It was well thought out and what they needed. Despite her initial scepticism, Rita saw value in the report, which would cost $3800. The only issue was that the couple had not felt any personal connection with the adviser, which they felt was important, given this would likely be a long-term relationship.

Meeting with Adviser 2

Pino and Rita subsequently went to see another adviser, who took them through a similar process, provided similar analysis and offered an SoA at a similar cost. However, their experience with this adviser was very different.

This second adviser did two things that separated him from the first. He explained why he was an adviser in the first place, what had motivated him to get into this profession and why he wanted to help make a difference to his clients' lives. This resonated with Pino and Rita, making them more comfortable that they knew a little of who this person was.

Second, while this adviser asked similar questions about their financial situation, he was genuinely interested in their own motivations. To Pino, he said, 'I can see you have worked really hard in this small business of yours, and no doubt put in long hours. It must be tough on you, Rita and your children, getting up early every morning and arriving home late every night. May I ask, then, what drives you to do what you do? What gets you out of bed every morning?'

Pino replied that while he was keen to build the business and make it worth selling to fund his retirement, his real motivation was to show his appreciation to his wife, Rita, who had always supported him in this venture when others said it was risky. She had had to make sacrifices. Five years from now, he planned to take Rita to Machu Picchu for their 25th wedding anniversary. This had been her number-one travel goal since she was a teenager.

'If I can do that, it will be my way of thanking her and all the hard work will have been worthwhile,' he said.

When Pino and Rita received a letter of engagement from this adviser, it summarised all the important options and strategies they had available to them, but it included a photo of Machu Picchu on the front cover and a savings strategy to ensure they could afford this goal, including flying business class.

Pino and Rita were left feeling that this adviser 'got them'. He understood that for them their plan would involve major emotional decisions. He did the numbers, of course, but it was the care factor that made the difference.

In dealing with any profession you get good and bad, or those who suit you but may not suit someone else. When looking for your own adviser, it's worth looking around to ensure you get the person who will work best for you and your family.

Glossary

Active fund—fund managers who buy and sell and actively manage the fund. This is a hands-on approach, unlike passive funds, which follow the market index to decide.

AFSL—the Australian Finance Services Licence is required to conduct a financial services business.

ASIC—the Australian Securities and Investments Commission is the federal government agency that enforces laws relating to companies, securities, financial services and credit, to protect consumers, investors and creditors.

Balanced fund—a multi-asset fund with a similar percentage of growth assets to defensive assets. A medium- to long-term time frame fund, it's preferred as the default fund for most employer super funds.

Beneficiaries—a person or estate, for example, nominated on an account, policy and/or a legal document to receive assets in the event of the owner's death.

Blue chip companies—well-established corporate businesses, usually listed on the sharemarket, which can potentially pay ongoing dividends.

BPAY—the shortened name for Bill Payment, which is an easy and secure payment service used in Australia to pay bills.

Capital gain—the increase in value of an asset from when it was originally purchased to when it is sold.

Capital gains tax (CGT)—when you sell an asset, the profit or capital gain made is taxable. The CGT reduces if you own the assets for more than a year.

Concessional contributions—contributions made into your superannuation account that are from pre-tax income and will be taxed at a lower rate.

Conservative fund—a multi-asset fund with a low percentage of growth assets (such as shares and property) and a high percentage of defensive assets (such as cash and bonds). A short-term time frame.

Deed of Enduring Guardianship—gives a selected individual the authority to make medical decisions on behalf of the person if they are unable to do so.

Dividends—an amount of money paid by a company to their shareholders from their profits.

Dollar cost averaging—an investment strategy of investing smaller fixed amounts over a certain amount of time instead of investing a lump sum. This reduces risk if the market fluctuates.

EFTPOS—the abbreviated name for Electronic Funds Transfer at Point of Sale. Refers to the electric fund payment method that allows the transfer of funds at the point of sale through a card payment.

Financial adviser or financial planner—an authorised representative of an AFSL licensed by the Australian Securities and Investments Commission (ASIC) who is able to provide advice on financial areas such as insurance, superannuation and investing.

Franking credit—a tax credit paid to company shareholders in addition to the dividends.

General insurance—refers to non-life insurance policies, such as car, pet and home insurance.

General insurance broker—a specialist in general insurance and risk management.

Government co-contribution—a contribution to an individual's superannuation account by the government to low- and middle-income earners.

Guarantor—a person who is allocated to a loan in case the owner of the loan is unable to repay it.

High growth fund—a multi-asset fund with a high percentage of growth assets of shares and property. A long-term time frame.

Income protection cover—an insurance policy that provides an income if you are unable to work due to illness or injury. The policy can pay up to 75 per cent of your gross income.

Index fund—a passive investment that track the sharemarket or another market index.

Insurance bond—a tax-paid investment with a range of investment options. Medium to long term.

Interest rate—how much money is earnt on an investment, or the amount of money owed on money borrowed, usually expressed as a percentage per annum.

Investment (or wrap) platforms—offer a range of investment options and services in one place. The platform provides administration and simplifies the process and management of the investment.

Investment property—properties that are purchased for investment with expected growth and rental income.

Life insurance cover—an insurance policy (can be called term insurance) which pays a lump sum in the event of the life insured's death. This is paid to the policy owner or nominated beneficiaries.

Managed investment fund—an investment fund where money from a range of investors is pooled together to be managed by a professional investment fund.

Mortgage—a type of loan or debt, normally against a home. Loans typically go for 25 years.

Negative gearing—when the expenses, such as the loan interest, are higher than the income earned, and can be tax deductible.

Non-concessional contributions—after-tax money paid as a contribution into a superannuation fund.

Power of Attorney—allows a person to act on behalf of another person for legal and financial matters. Can be enduring.

Risk adviser—a financial adviser/planner that specialises in life insurance advice and products.

Risk profile—used to evaluate a person's tolerance to risk versus the potential return, and to work out an appropriate mix of growth and defensive assets.

Salary sacrifice contributions—pre-tax salary to contribute to your superannuation fund over and above your Superannuation Guarantee Contributions (SGC).

Self-managed super fund (SMSF)—your own individual superannuation fund, which is your responsibility as trustee to run. Used for more control or for buying direct property, for example.

Spouse contributions—where the spouse (either married or de facto) contributes to their partner's super on their behalf.

Superannuation (super)—a government-legislated investment account for you to accumulate funds for your retirement in a tax-effective manner.

Superannuation Guarantee Contributions (SGC)—the minimum amount of money that your employer needs to pay to your super on your behalf. Currently set at 10 per cent per annum of your salary.

Term deposits—a bank account where a person can deposit funds for a set period such as six months or a year, for a fixed rate of return.

Total and permanent disability (TPD) insurance—a type of insurance that pays a lump sum if the life insured becomes permanently disabled due to an illness or injury.

Trauma (critical illness) insurance—a type of insurance that pays a lump sum if you suffer a critical illness such as cancer, heart disease or stroke. Does not need to be permanent, as with TPD.

Trust fund—a legal entity that puts assets (such as property or shares) in trust on behalf of another individual of group. A trustee creates the trust fund, and an appointor manages the trustee and the beneficiaries (who the trust fund was created for).

Will—a legal document for when someone dies, which provides instructions on how that person's estate is to be distributed.